Evaluating ELL Students for the Possibility of Special Education Qualification

2nd Edition

Steve Gill and Ushani Nanayakkara

Acknowledgments

We would like to thank the following people for their help during the editing of this book: Rebekah Hereth, Steve Hirsch, Tania May, and Patty Finnegan.

Also, a thank you goes out to everyone who has attended a training or contacted Steve to ask a question. These questions have been instrumental in helping us to learn and grow.

Table of Contents

Chapter 1: Introduction

I have spent much of my career looking for information on this topic and I have bought and read every single book I have come across on this topic. The majority of what I have read has been valuable, but much of it has been valuable on the systems level and not at the "boots on the ground" level. For example, many of the books focus on the changes needed at the systems level, like appropriate RTI/MTSS development. However, on the morning that I was writing this I was talking with a team in a state that is put forth as an exemplary state in the RTI work. I asked them what percentage of their schools do RTI well enough that they truly feel comfortable using that as a special education qualification model. The answer was 20%. Doing RTI or MTSS really well takes many moving pieces that are not the focus of this book. Instead, this book focuses on what the authors have learned in the years of working on this topic, and how an individual or team can understand and implement that knowledge in their building, their district, and their area.

This book focuses on data, belief systems, process, and the LE^{3}AP lens and then provides additional resources for the individuals completing evaluations. The additional resources focus on evidence that helps in the decision-making process, examples for reports, a checklist of minimum evidence, and recommended books.

Above, the terms RTI, MTSS and LE^{3}AP are used. RTI is an acronym for Response To Intervention, MTSS is Multi-Tiered Systems of Support, and LE^{3}AP is our acronym for Look at Exposure, Experience, Expectation and Practice. The LE^{3}AP will be explained in detail later in this book.

This Book Is Not

This book does not replace:

- District policy and/or practice in your area, unless your district adopts some or all of these concepts.
- State law requirements for your state.

This Book Is

- Meant to provoke thinking about the impact of experience, environment, expectations, and practice on presenting problems for each child individually.
- Meant to assist teams in building their processes.
- Meant to reduce over identification of language learners as students with disabilities.

Our goal is to make sure we are helping students to receive the services they need to be successful, to only qualify students for special education who truly have a disability that impacts their ability to access their education, and who need specially designed instruction directly correlated to the disability and adverse impact.

The Keys to Improvement at the School and Systems Level - The Process Needed to Increase Accuracy

In order for a school district to increase their accuracy of identifying the correct students for special education, who happen to be language learners, they should take the following steps. Please note, there are times in which the data is the necessary first step so that people take the belief systems work seriously. Other times the belief systems work is first to create a strong desire for people to know their data.

1. Belief Systems --- This may be our single biggest hurdle to overcome in achieving proportional qualification for all groups.
2. Data --- The schools and districts must analyze their data at the building and district level in order to look for disproportionalities and other problem areas. Then, the schools and districts need to have the difficult conversations in order to make plans that will address the disproportionalities and problems. This data needs to be examined at least once per year and methods/approaches modified as needed to achieve proportionate qualification and reduce or eliminate other problems.
3. Process --- The schools and districts need to adopt and utilize a process that helps them to gather and process the most critical data in a manner that leads to more proportionate results. The authors believe that the ELL Critical Data Process (K-12 and Preschool) fulfills this requirement and the feedback from numerous districts has been extremely positive regarding changing both perspectives and results. Washington State data provides strong evidence to support this process.
4. LE^{3}AP lens --- Our "lens" in which we view the world is impacted by our belief systems and our "lens" helps to create our belief systems. The LE^{3}AP lens is a method used to decrease the impact of our personal "lens."
5. New Knowledge --- The schools need to read and understand current literature that addresses concerns related to evaluating language learners for the possibility of special education services. The feedback on the ELL Critical Data Process book has been very positive as a tool to help teams. The book by Rhodes, Ochoa and Ortiz is also a very good book on the topic. There are only a handful of other books that the authors have found that provide useful suggestions that can be easily implemented. The authors also suggest that staff research the characteristics of the languages of students who are being referred for possible evaluation.

A Belief of the Authors

There is no doubt that disproportionality in special education has existed for at least 40 years and has changed little over those 40 years. Educators are good and caring people, because it certainly is not about the money. Knowing those two things, one must wonder why we have such discrepant numbers and results. We believe that we have been trained, in very subtle ways throughout our lives (acculturation), to have beliefs that we do not even know are there. And, "our" in the previous sentence means all of us. Incorrect or lacking knowledge combines with acculturation, to create flawed belief systems. The most subtle impacts of prejudice play themselves out in ways we are unaware of in our lives.

The following chapter focuses on the issues related to belief systems, to connect our acculturation (knowledge) to our belief systems, to our practices, and to our results. Our results are very poor in relationship to disproportionality, and we are not purposefully picking harmful practices. If we knew there was a problem with our belief systems we would have already dealt with that. The problems lie in our own acculturation and either incorrect or missing knowledge.

Why not qualify kids (who don't have disabilities) if it means that they will get extra help? This is a question that comes up again and again. This topic could fill another entire book. In short, if you qualify a student who does not have a disability for special education, you are stating that they have a disability to their teachers and parents. Eventually, the student is going to identify as a person with a disability. Their friends are going to identify them as someone with a disability. In most cases, this will lower the cognitive load of the work they are asked to complete and lower the expectations in general. They will be removed from the core instruction, usually 1-2 hours per day for the rest of their educational career, in order to receive a service they do not need, nor qualify for. This, in many or most cases, will impact the way they see themselves and the way the world sees them. In contrast, not qualifying a student who truly has a disability is robbing a student of a service they need to access their education. In other books, I have provided the data and research to show that the roughly 12% of students who are qualified for special education represents over qualification in general. I have data that represents millions of students across multiple states, and on average we qualify language learners about 50% MORE often than non-language learners. Therefore, it is unlikely that we are missing a large number of students who have disabilities and in contrast it is likely that we are qualifying a large number of students who do not have disabilities. Finally, many people have told me that they want the students qualified for special education to make sure they graduate from high school. That sounds good on the surface; however, the graduation rates that I have seen for students in general (systems level) is around 80% and the graduation rates for language learners and special education students is usually below 60%.

A Note About WAC and CFR

Within this book the Washington Administrative Code (WAC) has been quoted with regards to the laws. Steve has read the state laws for about a dozen states and the Code of Federal Regulations (CFR). All state special education laws are based on the CFR. States are expected to include the content of the CFRs and are allowed to add to the CFR but not subtract from the CFR. There are very famous examples of states trying to ignore/replace content from the CFR and always losing the battle. How the laws are written in each state does vary, but the core content of the CFR is within each of those versions.

Notes regarding terminology

The terms ESL (English as a Second Language) and LEP (Limited English Proficient) were the terms used when I first began studies in this area. Then, the term ELL (English Language Learner) became much more common. The term EL (English Learner) is becoming the more common term, but does not appear to be used or known across the country, yet. Our book is using the term ELL, in part because our ELL Critical Data Process was created prior to the likely change from ELL to EL. Another topic that can create confusion is the usage of the words native language, primary language, and home language. The term native language is defined in the law, yet that definition has changed during my career and might change again. The point is that we need to know what languages exist within the home, how they are used, and what language or languages our student of concern is using and experiences.

Chapter 2: Belief Systems

The journey along the way of working on ELL and Special Education issues has solidified my belief that our single biggest hurdle to overcome in achieving proportional qualification for all groups is belief systems in general. I have heard Clay Cook (a leader in RTI/MTSS work) and Anthony Muhammed (a leader in achievement gap work) both talk about finding belief systems change to be the key to success in their areas of expertise. There is no doubt that educators are good and caring people. There is no doubt that our intentions are good intentions. However, our results in the area of disproportionality are very poor and have remained very poor since the data was first measured.

Therefore, if people are not purposefully doing things that lead to poor results in these areas for our children, then something is occurring at the belief systems level. The problem is, if we knew what was wrong with our belief systems, we would have long since already corrected it. A big problem, though, is that we need to see our data, our proof, our results in order to know and understand there really is a problem in our own system, our own schools, where we work.

If the problem is at the belief systems level and we don't know which beliefs are causing the problems, then we need to examine our own acculturation and our own knowledge in order to figure this out. We will then find out where our subtle biases are, we will find out what parts of our knowledge are wrong, and we will find out what knowledge we are missing in order to do our best for our children.

The following pages provide insights into belief systems issues, through research, evidence, and stories.

Our Personal Journey

We are all experiencing our own personal journey, and everyone's journey is unique. Learning how to determine whether or not a student needs more interventions, or if a special education referral is more appropriate, is a long learning journey, and one that Steve is still traveling. This journey is made easier or more difficult depending upon each person's willingness and ability to reflect upon their acculturation (and knowledge), their beliefs, their actions (practices) and their results.

We are acculturated from the day we start to understand what is occurring around us. Acculturation is combined with knowledge and this creates belief systems that eventually lead to actions and practices at work. Our practices lead to results, good, bad, or other. We know our results with regards to disproportionality are poor. Our results are not poor because we are actively and knowingly doing bad things (actions or practices), given educators are good and caring people. In order for us to achieve different results, we need to understand what is occurring with our belief systems and acculturation, and how these impact our practices. Then, we can modify our practices and achieve different results. Key questions each person needs to ask themselves, whatever the problem might be, are: "Am I part of creating or maintaining this problem? Or am I part of solving the problem? Our results on disproportionality are very poor, what is my role? Can I possibly know the answer if I don't know the data for my school, district, and state?" Highly unlikely!

One principal that Steve worked with told him, "all of my best teachers are worried about not doing enough and not doing a good enough job and all of my weakest teachers believe they have nothing to learn and think they are working harder than everyone else." We (the authors) believe that when there is a situation at work (or in life) in which things do not go right or do not go well, the very first thoughts should be about the following: What could I have done differently? What could I have done better? What can I learn from this? This mindset is likely to lead to learning from our mistakes and remaining a learner throughout our career (and life for that matter).

Therefore, each of us needs to examine our belief systems and our acculturation, so we understand if we are helping to create some of the disproportionality or if we are part of maintaining existing disproportionality. This process is difficult and at times painful. However, it is necessary for us to figure out how we can be part of the solution, a goal each and every one of us should strive to achieve.

The following pages are meant to provoke thinking and to provide you with examples to help stimulate others' thinking. Hopefully this will also evoke emotions, as emotions help us to remember what we have learned. For example: a parent may try to teach their 3-4-year-old a new word that isn't important to the child, and the child just does not learn the new word. But when the parent gets cut off by another driver and responds, "$ *&^ @#$ $#@#," the child, only having heard this phrase once, uses it the following day in the correct context, with correct intonation, and with emotion. Don't forget, this will happen in front of your parents, or friends.

So, as you read this, think about:

Acculturation → Belief Systems → Practices → Results

Results→ Practices → Belief Systems → Acculturation

Think about whether you are a part of creating, maintaining, or fixing the problems in your system, and what evidence you have to support your view of where you stand in your system. We are good and caring people, we can use the emotions to fuel a desire to learn more, change our practices, and support others to change their practices.

Our results occur not by chance, but as a result of our practices. Our practices occur based upon what we believe in and our belief systems are a combination of our knowledge and our acculturation. How we are acculturated creates a lens through which we see the world.

The stories in the following pages provide examples of this. We are sharing these with you to build knowledge and to encourage you to continuously monitor and challenge personal beliefs and practices.

Overview

1) **We See What We Are Acculturated To See:** Real world examples of acculturation creating a lens.
2) **Steve's Personal Educator Journey:** Real world example of developing over time, making mistakes, gaining new knowledge, learning, changing practices.
3) **Steve Hirsch's and Walter Gilliam's Research:** Research that shows the impact of our biases.
4) **Monolingual Nation:** Real world examples that help us see what could be unrealistic expectations and/or a lack of reasonable expectations.
5) **Literacy and Intelligence:** Knowledge to help us see things differently.
6) **Poverty:** Research that shows our results, and indicates biases.
7) **Qualification Versus Disability:** Research that shows that our results do not follow logical patterns, nor our "spoken" beliefs.
8) **Reading and Referrals:** Research that indicates our system, results and beliefs have significant flaws.
9) **Impact of Race on Qualification Rates:** Research that shows our results, again, do not follow logical patterns, nor our "spoken" beliefs
10) **Qualification Does Not Equal Disability:** A summary of data and research that show how unlikely it is that qualification rate actually equals disability rate in our system.

Then, the chapter ends with a write-up regarding the "takeaways" for each of these areas.

1. We See What We Are Acculturated to See

The following three examples are meant to help you understand that we see what we are acculturated to see. Our acculturation provides a lens which we look through and that changes our view of the world.

Ushani is one of the few people on earth who is a German/Sri Lankan. Sri Lanka is an island in the Indian Ocean, just south of India. Therefore, it's easy to assume that Germans and Sri Lankans do not commonly meet one another in such a way that relationships are likely to begin. Additionally, of the Germans and Sri Lankans who do meet, not all of them speak a common language. Then, of the Germans and Sri Lankans who do meet and who do speak a common language, not very many are likely to form a romantic relationship, get married, and have children.

People who meet Ushani struggle greatly in figuring out her heritage and make many assumptions. Ushani has had numerous experiences in which someone has spoken Spanish to her, assuming that she is a Latina, only to have Steve respond. This tends to leave the person completely dumbfounded. They probably wonder why the Latina* doesn't speak Spanish, but the older white guy does (some folks have literally told Steve that it is confusing to them to have an older white guy speaking Spanish with them). When Ushani is around people who are Black or African American, she is often thought to be a light skinned Black or African American woman. Then, there are times in which people believe that Ushani is a woman from India (to her Sri Lankan relatives, this is totally illogical). Virtually no one guesses that Ushani is from Sri Lanka. This is in large part because people rarely have a mental picture of what someone from Sri Lanka looks like (a lack of knowledge, a lack of this being part of one's acculturation). Did you have a picture of what someone from Sri Lanka might look like prior to this? Nobody ever guesses German, and many Germans have struggled to "see" Ushani as a German. Some Germans think she is Turkish; others think she is Black. A friend of the family once asked her mother when she considered moving back to Germany, "Don't you think it will be difficult for a Black child to grow up in Germany?"

People are not acculturated to see someone who looks like Ushani as German. Acculturation created lenses for each of these groups that impacted their decision making and their actions, like it does for all of us.

*Steve usually uses the terms Latino(a) and Black, instead of Hispanic and African-American, given his acculturation. This is an important point about cultural competence versus cultural responsiveness that we will discuss near the end of this chapter.

The following example from Steve's experience as a child with an extreme speech impediment and aphasia illustrates how acculturation and belief systems can create lenses through which people interpret the world.

Steve's grandmother told him the following story many times. When Steve was 3 to 4 years old, Steve's parents were convinced by their friends that he must be "retarded," the term of the time. Eventually, his parents took him to Seattle Children's Hospital for an evaluation. The first person who saw Steve was a Speech and Language Pathologist, and this person told Steve's parents that not only was he not "retarded," he might actually be bright. That same afternoon Steve was evaluated by either Nancy or Hal Robinson (The Robinson Center on the University of Washington Campus) and Steve's parents were told he was gifted. A strange day in the life of a child who had no idea what was going on. The jury is still out regarding who was right (that is meant to be funny ☺).

During the time Steve's parents were convinced by others that he might be "retarded," at an age of 3-4 years old, Steve was reading and playing chess with adults. Most folks were sure Steve was just looking at the books and they didn't believe his mother's claim that he was reading (given nobody could understand what he was saying). The chess was pretty hard to deny, since people could see it occur. So, why did people think he was "retarded?" As a child Steve could not effectively communicate and was therefore seen by others to be cognitively limited, or "dumb." In our society, people who don't speak English are often seen as unlikely to be intelligent*. However, in our schools with language learners, it is possible that the smartest child in the school does not yet speak English.

*Steve has noticed during his training events that people in the audience who speak English as a second or later language all nod their heads in agreement when this point is made.

Have you ever seen an interview with Tiger Woods in which he talks about how much it bothers him that he is virtually never seen as an Asian man? Do you ever think of Tiger Woods as an Asian man? Or, solely as a Black or African American man? Tiger Woods expresses how he sees this as disrespectful to his mother and the heritage he has inherited from her.

There are many other examples in our world, yet this provides a window into how acculturation creates a lens through which we view our world. We need to examine ourselves to see how our acculturation is creating our lens.

2. Steve's Personal Educator Journey: The Painful Life Lessons

When Steve was in graduate school there was no coursework on the assessment of language learners; it was not even discussed. Steve began his career in the Tacoma School District and he quickly realized that he lacked skills in the area of evaluating language learners. Then he learned that finding information on this topic was next to impossible. This was pre-Google.

The first event to shape Steve's experience was a little boy who walked into his office with a doctor's script that said "ADHD, qualifies for special education as a student with an Other Health Impairment." School psychologists often do not take this any better than medical doctors would take school psychologists making medical diagnosis and sending the families to the doctor's office. Steve called the doctor and asked him how he made the diagnosis, and the doctor responded, "I was educated at Harvard." After hearing this a few times Steve expressed his lack of care regarding the doctor's education. The doctor finally said, "I interviewed the family." Steve responded, "You speak Vietnamese?" The doctor then told Steve to do things that would be anatomically difficult to achieve, Steve responded, and eventually the doctor hung up the phone (it is likely Steve was having a better time than the doctor). It was later discovered that this student did not have ADHD and the family had no idea what had occurred.

Steve moved on with his career, eventually landing in a district that had a large percentage of Spanish speaking students in special education. Steve decided that he wanted to be bilingual and biliterate, so he started taking night classes. After a year, he might have achieved the ability to ask where the bathroom is or order a beer, but not much more. With a great deal of luck, Steve ended up eating dinner with Dr. Stephen Krashen, one of the leading experts in the world on language acquisition. Dr. Krashen told Steve what he needed to do, and it was all about comprehensible input. So, Steve started to read books in Spanish, starting with kindergarten level books, until he mastered those, then first grade level books, and when he mastered those, second grade level books (reading The Mouse and the Motorcycle with great excitement), and so on.

Steve eventually had a dilemma. The only books at his level that he could find were the Twilight series, something rather hard on his ego (please note, this story is going somewhere). Steve thought he was safe reading this at school, and was walking to the staff lounge holding this book when a nice little girl that Steve knew well asked him if she could borrow the book after he was done with it. Steve first thought "Why?" believing she could not read the book because she was qualified for special education for reading, had never lived in a Spanish speaking country, and had no formal education in Spanish. Steve told her, "I will buy you brand new copies of the books if you stop by my office each week to, 1) Tell me about what you read, 2) Tell me about what you liked, 3) Tell me about what you think will happen next." This did not go as Steve thought it would go. Not only did she read every one of these books, she provided Steve replies to his questions ad nauseam. The point to this story is that not only was she qualified for special education for reading in English, not only had she never been formally educated in Spanish, not only was she reading at a higher level in Spanish than in English, Steve was the school psychologist who had qualified her for special education. This was a painful learning moment for Steve. A moment that required a lot of reflection.

Soon after this Steve began working for the Kent School District as the ESA Coach (the coach for all of the school psychologists, speech and language pathologists, occupational therapists, and physical therapists). He was offered the opportunity to attend the district supported ELL graduate level program through Heritage University. This is where the work on the ELL Critical Data Process began, and the puzzle pieces started coming together.

The point of these stories is that each of us is on a journey of skills development. This can only occur if each of us is honest with ourselves about our mistakes, honest with ourselves regarding the impact of our acculturation, honest with ourselves about our skills (or lack of skills), honest with ourselves about our knowledge (or lack of knowledge) and if we do something to work on our own issues (Yoda said, "There is no try, there is do and not do"). We also need to be willing to examine our own issues around belief systems and race, in order to improve and focus on making a difference in disproportionality.

15

3. Steve Hirsch's Research

Steve Hirsch is a school psychologist in Washington State who has been a leader within the state school psychologist association for many years. Dr. Hirsch completed the following research as part of other ongoing projects and presented the information at the state school psychologist conference, trying to help people understand that we have biases that we are not aware of, and that those biases are impacting our work. The slides below represent the results after staff were given identical data on four students, in which the only difference was the name of the student and the country of origin.

The first slide below shows that, with identical data, the Latino students were significantly more likely to be referred for special education evaluations. The second slide, with identical data for each of the students, shows that there are significantly different rates of recommendation to complete an early re-evaluation for the possibility to exit the student from special education, based solely upon their race (based upon the subtle and likely unknown biases of the participants).

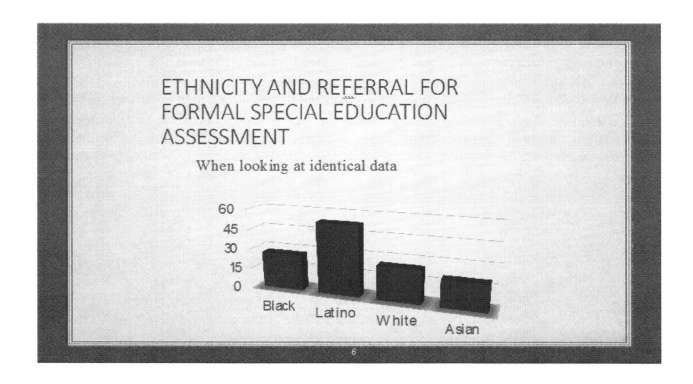

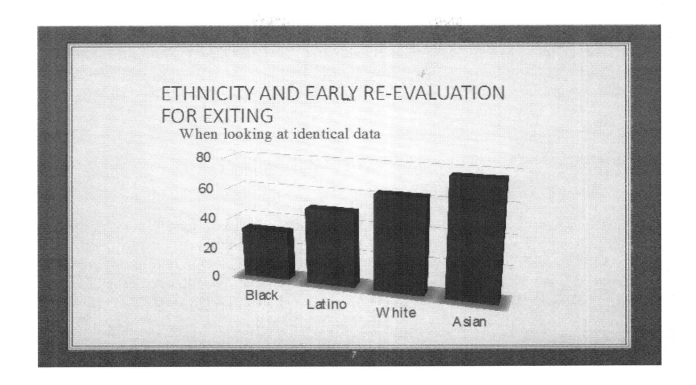

We all want to believe that we do not have biases, yet we all have them. It is a natural part of being human. We need to have the courage to examine our biases and the impact of those upon our work.

Dr. Hirsch noted the following in an email to Steve when he was commenting on the second edition draft of this book, "My follow-up with 250+ Washington school psychologists yielded the same results." We all have biases!

Another excellent example of research on biases is the research completed at Yale University by lead researcher Walter Gilliam. This research had a group of teachers watching videos of children playing, and they were asked to identify the challenging behaviors as they saw them occur in the videos. There were four children, one White boy, one White girl, one Black boy, and one Black girl. The researchers used eye scanning technology to watch the eyes of the teachers. The teachers watched the Black boys significantly more than the other children. The interesting part is that there was no challenging behavior at all occurring in the videos. The research has other very important components and is well worth reading (if you Google Walter Gilliam and research on biases you will find this and other research written about in many articles). Black boys are identified as behaviorally disabled at a much higher rate than other children. What if that is a result of school staff expecting them to behave poorly, watching them more closely than other children, and reacting differently given those expectations? Is it also possible that these children behave differently because they feel that they are being treated unfairly, singled out?

One of the readers of this second edition noted that the research shows that we are also misinterpreting the behaviors of the black children to reflect meanings that just are not true. This equates well with a quote from the Talmud, "We don't see the world how it is, we see the world how we are."

4. Monolingual Nation: Our Expectations of Our Students

Are we really the "monolingual" nation???

Are our expectations of our students based upon knowledge of the challenges that they face? And, do we have any personal experience related to the depth of those challenges? We have created the following food for thought. First, however, a small joke: What do you call someone who speaks 3 or more languages? Multilingual. What do you call someone who speaks 2 languages? Bilingual. What do you call someone who speaks just one language? American…. ☺

Steve was studying in Valencia, Spain, in a large language school. There were over 100 students, mostly from Northern Europe. There were only 2 Americans, and both Americans were receiving a LARGE quantity of negativity regarding Americans and Americans' ethnocentricity. "You people don't even care enough to learn another language." After about a week of this, Steve responded (in a nice way) that he had had enough. Eventually after more commentary, Steve pointed out that they used their best English speakers/writers to create signs in English and every single one of the signs had an error. They originally thought this was impossible. Steve, at their urging, took them around the building to every sign with English text and explained the errors (all the signs had errors). This eventually became a game, with all the students who were attempting to learn English taking Steve around the campus to talk about every sign they could find.

In Sri Lanka, in the big city of Colombo, it is not difficult to find someone who speaks English (it is very common throughout the schools to teach English). During one of their trips Steve and Ushani stayed in a hotel outside of Colombo. The hotel stated that it would always have someone available who spoke English. One day Steve and Ushani needed some towels, and went to the front desk. The front desk sent for the person who could speak English. Steve and Ushani then worked with this person for quite some time trying to express what they needed (this could have been a Saturday Night Live skit, or a Candid Camera scene).

After visiting Sri Lanka, Steve and Ushani visited Ushani's family in Germany. After a few days, Steve told Ushani she didn't need to interpret any longer for him, he was content to just smile and nod his head. Have you ever noticed a language learner looking at you, smiling and nodding their head? Have you ever done this with your spouse, significant other, or a good friend when you didn't understand the topic that they kept talking about? Do you know what that means? It means they (or you) got tired of concentrating and trying to make sense of what the others were saying and chose to just nod and smile.

The point to this story is not to pick on any other group, but to challenge the ideas that everyone else speaks multiple languages, that everyone speaks English, and that speaking a little bit of another language is being bilingual or multilingual. The point is that we are not just expecting our English Language Learners to know something about their family's store or business, we are not expecting them to hold simple conversations. Instead, we are expecting them to function on high stakes tests. And, if they do not function well on these tests we wonder whether or not they have a disability....

Camino de Santiago

This sign in Spanish and English is an example of the type of sign seen in Spain. It is highly unlikely that anyone who speaks only English would understand what they are facing along this path. The English should say:

Attention Cyclists

Steep Hills in/for 15 kilometers

Ride with caution.

Without actually being on the path it is impossible to know if the sign is meant to say "in" 15 kilometers or "for" 15 kilometers. Spanish speakers and readers, why would they have a sign that warns bicyclists about a something that is an hour away (if you believe it means "in" 15 kilometers)?

How many of you studied Spanish in high school and/or college? Some of you for years, right? Why couldn't you understand what the sign said? Because, it just is not that easy to reach a functional level in a second or higher language. Do you expect your English Language Learners to function at this level or higher? If they don't, do they get referred for a possible special education evaluation? How many years and what levels of support are they given, prior to a judgment that their progress just is not good enough…?

5. Literacy and Intelligence

A belief held here in the United States is that people who cannot read are on average of lower intelligence. There could be some correlation in countries with exceptionally high rates of literacy. However, some knowledge is needed to reduce the overgeneralization of this belief. There are roughly 7,000 languages on Earth and about 100 years ago only an estimated 2,000 of these languages had a written system. Some of the remaining 5,000 languages had written forms, but very few people knew them. Over the last 100 years, people from these 5,000 or so languages have in many cases worked very hard to create a written form for their language (or a standardized and agreed upon form of their language), fearing that the language would be "lost" if it did not have a known, documented and used written form. Some of these languages have only had a written form for roughly 50 years.

The Kent School District is in King County (along with Seattle). Within King County there is a very large Somali population. What we have read about the Somali language indicates that there were 5-6 written forms for Somali that were not widely known or widely used. Then, in the late 1960's a new written form was agreed upon. Given how young this written form is, the literacy rate in Somali is currently estimated at under 30%. There are many languages that are in this same place right now. Therefore, in situations like this, a lack of reading skill is more likely related to a lack of exposure, experience, expectation and practice. And, in situations like this, a lack of reading skills is not likely to be related to intelligence or a learning disability.

6. Poverty

When working with large groups of educators and asking the following question, rarely is there someone who is willing to raise their hand and say "yes:"

Do people in poverty have higher rates of disabilities?

The answer is yes, but not based upon what some people might be thinking. The answer is yes because people with disabilities have higher rates of poverty. Reading deficits exist with roughly 80% of all students in special education. In our country, someone who cannot read, on average, is going to have a much more difficult time obtaining a living wage job. Therefore, there is some causation from disability to poverty, and a small correlation of poverty to higher rates of disability. Sadly, though, the research shows that students in poverty are frequently over identified for special education even though the correlations/causations noted above are about their parents and not about our students. And, poverty does not cause disabilities, but instead can be linked to less exposure and experience, and sometimes less time for parent support. These factors do not make a student disabled, but instead create a situation in which a student is likely to have a more difficult time in school. The following pages document the research Steve completed in Washington State, showing that our qualification rates and our poverty rates are linked, sadly.

7. Qualification vs. Disability

Special Education Qualification Rates in Washington State and the Link to Free and Reduced Lunch Rates

Steve examined the data for 295 school districts. No district was purposely left out of the data, with the exception of school districts in the data set that were(are) not actually comprehensive school districts (e.g., School for the Blind). Therefore, with a set of 250 districts, it is highly unlikely that any district missed would have impacted the noted trends.

For 16 districts the special education eligibility percentages fell below 10% of the total student population. For 15 of these 16 school districts, the average student population in the districts was 145 students (145 is the average of the total student population and not just the total for the special education population; the 16th was a medium sized district noted separately below).

There were 32 districts with special education eligibility percentages above 18% of the total student population. The average student population across these districts was 392 students. As above, 392 represents the total student population and not just the special education population. The highest percentage of children qualified as children with disabilities was 37.5% of the district. Can there really be a district where 37.5% of the children have disabilities? That district happened to have a population in which 75% of the students were of Native American heritage. Did those two numbers happen together totally by chance? That is very unlikely and the results are highly likely to be inappropriate.

In the State of Washington, 45.9% of the students were on Free or Reduced Lunch at the time of this research. The average percentage of F/R Lunch for the districts below 10% special education qualification rate was 24%. The average percentage of F/R Lunch for the districts above 18% was 75.6%.

The only medium/large district with a percentage below 10% of the student population qualified for special education services was the Issaquah School District, at 8.8%. It is interesting to note that Issaquah School District has some of the highest state test scores noted during this research.

Although the F/R Lunch difference is extreme, there is no way to prove that it is a causal factor. Yet, many research studies have indicated that poverty is a very high predictor of special education qualification. This occurs even though it would be very hard to argue, beyond a minimal percentage difference, that poverty has any correlation to rates of disabilities, and no causal relationship either. It is important to note that the causal or correlational issues we are talking about are the parents of our children, not our children. Therefore, the correlation becomes even far weaker when looking at the children. That is, the small correlation of the parent in poverty to disability of the parent would be multiplied by the small correlation of parent to child disability (inheritance) to achieve a very small correlational value/predictive value.

It is interesting to note that virtually all of the districts on the extremes of the range have very small student populations. In all of these cases, one or only a few people are leading the qualification decisions. However, a group of people are at the table each time, sustaining or solving the problem (or creating it in some cases). What table are you sitting at? How do you know? Do you have data to prove your perception?

It would be hard to examine this data and not see the human impact on the work. We have a lot of power in influencing outcomes, and, hopefully, a lot to think about in our daily work to bring about positive student outcomes.

You will see these points repeated throughout the book because we have a very hard time seeing ourselves involved in any of the negative results ("we" being that universal we). However, most staff have not examined the data for their schools and district. We need to have the courage to look closely at our work and to begin to solve problems as they appear. The data is not the way it is because so few people are involved in the problem. Wherever there is a problem, a lot of staff members were involved in creating or maintaining the problem (remember, not bad people, just bad results). This could seem to contradict what was said above. However, in the problem noted above just a few people had "control" over the outcome, yet many people had input and involvement. So, the big "we" could have stopped the problem if they had seen it as a problem. We need as many people as possible involved in the solutions.

The following quote from the University of Texas at Austin is included to provide additional insight into this issue.

Education and Transition to Adulthood, Information on Learning Disabilities, available at: http://www.utexas.edu/cola/etag/Related%20Sites/Learning-Disabilities.php

> *Although the research focus has primarily been on the disproportionate labeling of racial minorities with LD, the research team found that differences in the rates of being labeled are more dramatic by socioeconomic status (SES) than by race. The odds of being labeled with LD are much higher among low SES than high SES high school students, regardless of whether the student is Black or white. In fact, low SES white high school students are as likely as low SES Black or Hispanic high school students to be labeled with LD, but much greater proportions of racial minorities are in that high-risk low SES group.*

> *In contrast to Black and white high school students, high SES Hispanic high school students are as likely as low SES Hispanic high school students to be labeled with LD. The team found that disproportionate labeling of Hispanic*

students with learning disabilities in high school is attributable to the over-labeling of language minorities.

The team also found that students attending higher poverty schools are actually less likely to be labeled with LD, and that systematic differences in academic achievement by SES, race, and linguistic status are a major factor in disproportionality.

Underline added for emphasis.

8. Reading and Referrals

Qualification rates are not equivalent to disability rates

Schools and systems using RTI or MTSS with fidelity have higher test scores and lower rates of disability qualification. We are using this as evidence of over qualification, along with Carnine's research and the SLD research (like the work of Dr. Torgesen from Florida).

Specific Learning Disability is a category that was, more or less, created for the special education world. It is the only category that greatly increased beyond population change from 1975 to 2004, when the special education population in the United States peaked between 2000 and 2004, and has since been dropping. It is the main category to decrease in size since 2004. The SLD category tripled in numbers from 1975 to 2004, eventually being the category in which roughly 50% of all special education students were qualified. Interestingly enough, the decrease in this category started with the federal law that included the usage of RTI qualification. It is easy to see the decrease in the SLD category aligning with the increased usage of RTI within the school systems. At last check, SLD now represents roughly 38.8% of all students qualified for special education. (This was written in 2017 looking at the most current Office of Special Education Programs (OSEP) published data).

The following quotes provide a lot to think about and are followed by ways to mitigate these concerns.

Dr. Carnine (University of Oregon) testifying to the Senate
  ▶ "Moving to a response to intervention model can dramatically reduce the long-term failure that is often associated with the IQ-achievement discrepancy formula. 70 to 90 percent of the most at risk children in Kindergarten through 2nd grade can be brought to the average range with effective instruction."

The research into well-implemented RTI or Tiered Intervention has shown that many students who would have previously qualified under SLD have been appropriately served (and have better long-term outcomes) through interventions implemented within the general education setting.

Dr. Torgesen from Florida

> "Within 1 year following the intervention, 40% of the children were found to be no longer in need of special education services."
> This was only 8 weeks of intervention at 2 hours per day and the children were labeled "with severe reading disabilities…"

Whether looking at this research or the research on the Lindamood-Bell approach, it is easy to see that short-term intensive intervention that is focused on the specific needs of the children shows us that many children do not have disabilities, but instead are casualties of our system. The research noted above was with children considered to have "severe reading disabilities." Studies show that similar methods with students who would be considered to have mild reading disabilities have results of up to 80% of students no longer needing special education services. Think about the implications. What if 50% of all students in special education do not actually have disabilities and actually just need intensive interventions (taking the 80% of SLD students and adding a small error rate in the other categories that are "soft")?

Is this really happening???

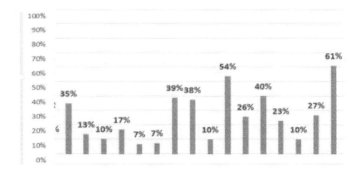

A snapshot of one district's data…. Percentage ELL qualified for special education by building

The graph above is from one of the school districts that Steve worked with on ELL and Special Education Issues. However, Steve has seen this same type of data across all of the districts who have provided data, and for both ELL and non-ELL students (some not as severe, some worse, all with unexplainable (via logic) results). Some of this is caused by small data sets and how they can provide results that are more random than real. However, this type of pattern is so consistent that the problem is beyond small sample size issues. Even after subtracting out small sample problems, this type of graph shows that whether or not a student qualifies for special education can change depending upon the school they are in at the time. This is more information to show staff that qualification rates do not equal disability rates.

What if students are not getting their needs met?

RTI and ELLs

ELL students in schools that do not have an "RTI" model in place are 3 times as likely to be identified for special education.

Source --- Rhodes, Ochoa, Ortiz

Intervention versus Qualification for Special Education....

The quote above from Rhodes, Ochoa and Ortiz is very similar to the data from districts Steve has worked with.

The districts that do not provide targeted interventions in a systematic manner frequently have 2 to 3 times as many ELL students qualified for special education services (when compared to non-ELL students). Given that special education qualification rates across the nation are usually in the 12-13% range, ask yourself whether or not you believe that it is possible that 24-39% (a range from 2 x 12% to 3 x 13%) of any group could possibly all have a disability? Is your district one of these districts? Are you part of maintaining, creating or solving the problem? In contrast, there are schools who have high rates of success on state and national testing and they frequently have much lower rates of special education qualification. In the Kent School District, the three highest performing schools at the time of writing this book had special education qualification rates of 2.5%, 5%, and 6%.

Washington State Data

Eligibility rate of Special Education for all Students is 13.3%

Eligibility rate of Special Education for Language Learners is 19.7%

There are 31 districts whose percentage is from 26.6% to 39.9%

There are 8 districts whose percentage is from 40%-50%

There are 2 districts whose percentage is above 50%

There are only 22 districts, out of 295 whose eligibility rate for language learners is at or below the state average for all students. The Kent School District is one of those 22 school districts.

The above slide was created for trainings that Steve provides from the state department data. Comparing the 13.3% for all students to the 19.7% for language learners the reader can see that language learners are roughly 50% more likely than non-language learners to be qualified for special education services. Is there anyone who believes that the simple fact of not yet speaking English well increases your likelihood of having a disability? The reader can see that 41 districts qualified 26.6% to over 50% of their language learners for special education services. This ranges from the bizarre to the crazy!

In contrast, there are just 22 districts from the 295 school districts in Washington who qualify language learners at or slightly below the rate that children in general are qualified for special education services. Of these 22 districts, 19 of the 22 are very similar. These 19 districts are districts with low special education qualification in general, low rates of poverty, low rates of the general issues that tend to be directly related to problems with disproportionality. Within those 19, though was one district who had disproportionality in the past. Their director of ELL services recently told me that they believe that full implementation of the ELL Critical Data Process was the primary reason for their improvement. The remaining 3 are the Kent School District (where Steve first rolled out the ELL Critical Data process and worked until 2018) and two other districts.

That led to a need to research the remaining three districts to better understand the results. The Kent School District is often referred to as the most diverse district in Washington and one of the most diverse in the United States. The Kent School District has one of the three largest

ELL student populations within Washington with nearly 6,000 language learners. Also, the Kent School District has, on average, over 130 languages spoken by our students. The two other districts had a very high percentage of Hispanic students (something that is often correlated to over qualification) and higher rates of Free and Reduced Lunch. Within these districts, though, there was the highest rate of Hispanic teachers that Steve has seen during his work. Research has shown that the rate of disproportionality decreases with the increase in teacher population matching student population (see quote later in this book).

Education Week on Disproportionality

"... African-American students were nearly or greater than twice as likely as white students to be classified with emotional or intellectual disabilities

In other words, there are kids who are placed in these programs because educators either don't want to deal with them, don't know how to deal with them, or don't know how to be responsive to them.

Scholars generally don't blame racial disproportionality in special education on outright discrimination. Instead, they say it typically derives from systemic flaws within a school or district's instructional culture that allow for some disadvantaged students to fall through the cracks."

Keeping Special Ed in Proportion, by Anthony Rebora, available at:
http://www.edweek.org/tsb/articles/2011/10/13/01disproportion.h05.html

Our problems are not about bad people doing bad things, given educators are good and caring people doing their best. The poor results as noted in the quote above and the following quote are about systems level flaws that usually can be traced back to unconscious bias (our acculturation and our belief systems) and a lack of knowledge (what to do differently).

Report to Congress on Disproportionality

Using data from the U.S. Department of Education, analyses suggest that Black children are 2.88 times more likely than White children to be labeled as having mental retardation and 1.92 times more likely to be labeled as having an emotional/behavioral disorder (Losen & Orfield, 2002). Research suggests that unconscious racial bias, stereotypes, inequitable implementation of discipline policies, and practices that are not culturally responsive may contribute to the observed patterns of identification and placement for many minority students."

Information from the *Twenty-fourth Annual Report to Congress on the Implementation of the Individuals with Disabilities Education Act (IDEA)* (U.S. Department of Education, 2002), available at: http://www2.ed.gov/about/reports/annual/osep/2002/index.html

SLD qualification has fallen from 50% to 38.8% while RTI and MTSS have gone up

The percentage of special education students qualified using SLD used to be about 50% of all students in special education. The usage of SLD peaked between 2000 and 2004, and has consistently been dropping since 2004. As of last available OSEP data (as this was written), Specific Learning Disability went from being 50% of all special education student to 38.8%. At the same time the usage of RTI and MTSS has increased. Is there anyone who believes that this is a coincidence? If we agree that this is not a coincidence, it is evidence that our belief systems were impacting our decisions, and still are, given that 38.8% is a very large number. We didn't just say let's put the kids into special education to get them some extra help, we said that the students had disabilities.

80% of referrals are about reading

We know that roughly 80% of students in special education have reading as a service, in many cases the primary service. We know that Dr. Carnine's meta-analysis of RTI/MTSS work shows that 70%-90% of the students we would like to qualify for special education in the 2nd or 3rd grade are not in need of qualification after they receive appropriate interventions. We know from the work of Dr. Torgesen and the research on Lindamood-Bell work, as high as 80% of the students with reading "disabilities" can be brought to grade level with short-term intense intervention. We know that in many, possibly most cases, special education services within any given district encumbers upon general education funding (special education does not get enough money to pay its own bills). Disability is within quotes above, given that it is hard to imagine something being a disability if 8-10 weeks of intervention can eliminate the problem.

So, what if a large number of students could be brought to grade level with the appropriate early interventions or short-term intense interventions? We would not only save money, we would also have students finding more success. We mentioned earlier that the three top-performing elementary schools in Kent have very low rates of special education qualification (and, these are not high SES schools). Also, a school district south of Kent was just recognized as having the fastest achievement gap closure in the state (they are also one of the only school districts using RTI as a districtwide method of special education qualification in Washington). These things cannot all be happening by chance!!!

The following information is taken from a presentation that Dr. Joseph Torgesen provided called "A Scientific Success Story: Specific Reading Disabilities or Developmental Dyslexia" at the Florida Council for Exceptional Children, October 2006.

Dr. Torgesen reported on an intensive intervention provided for 60 students who had severe reading disabilities. The children were between 8 and 10 years of age. They had been receiving special education services for an average of 16 months. They were considered the worst readers and were on average at least 1.5 S.D. below grade level. They had standard scores of 69 for Word Attack, 69 for Word Identification and had Verbal IQs of 93 (average for each of these). These students were randomly assigned to two different groups and explicitly taught phonics skills. Both groups of students received 67.5 hours of one-to-one instruction, 2 hours per day for 8 weeks. The students were followed for two years after the intervention was completed.

The results of the work are the following. The students not only gained skills that placed them in the average range, they actually continued to increase their reading skills after the intervention, scoring higher on standardized testing 2 years after the post intervention testing than at the post intervention testing. This means that they didn't just make initial gains, they didn't just maintain those gains, they improved relative to their peers over time. Dr. Torgesen then asked the question, "How do we make this kind of instruction available to every child who needs it?" Imagine the positive impact on our children, both short-term and long-term, if we achieved this! Imagine the positive impacts on our classrooms if we achieved this!

9. Impact of Race on Qualification Rates

Does anyone still believe that people from different races have different rates of disabilities? When Steve was working on the over identification of Black/African American students as students with intellectual disabilities, he was told the following more than once: "Everyone knows that Black/African American students have lower average IQs, which means there will be more with IQs below 70, and that is why we have more qualified for Intellectual Disabilities." This is no joke, people really said that and believed that. Sadly, this type of thinking was exacerbated due to a book called The Bell Curve. This book provides data that people take out of context and use inappropriately. Also, it is the belief of this author that the authors of The Bell Curve do not understand what factors can impact intelligence test scores. Again, belief

29

systems and acculturation have an impact on the way in which we see the world. For people who believe things like this, it is much easier for them to believe that their tests are an accurate representation if the results are poor. They are less likely to question their results and look for a different explanation/cause (most of these people are good and caring people, just in need of some new knowledge).

The quotes noted earlier show extreme disproportionality in our qualification rates of our Black/African American students. We say that we believe that the rate of disabilities does not differ by race, yet our qualification rates vary to the extreme for certain groups in certain categories. This is evidence that we need to examine our beliefs systems and acculturation. This is a complex topic, yet sincere and open conversations and reflection are needed to find our way to better results.

The following quote from the Center for Public Education is included to provide further evidence on this topic.

> *"The disparities between whites and some minorities in special education appear mostly in the categories with the most subjective eligibility criteria, such as "mild mental retardation" or "specific learning disabilities." Many believe the disproportionate representation is due to misconceptions about race and culture, and that Black and Hispanic children are more likely to be misidentified as disabled (Education Week 2004, National Research Council 2002).*

For instance, Matthew Ladner and Christopher Hammons argue that race plays an enormously important role in how students are identified as disabled (Ladner and Hammons, 2001). In a study in the book *Rethinking Special Education for a New Century,* they found that in districts with a predominantly Black faculty, there was a reduction in minority student enrollment in special education services by three to four times. "Race," they concluded, "impacts special education rates far more than any other variable."

This examination of special education was prepared for the Center for Public Education by Ulrich Boser, October 15, 2009, available at:

http://www.centerforpubliceducation.org/Main-Menu/Evaluating-performance/Special-education-At-a-glance/Special-education-A-better-perspective-full-report.html

On a related note: Is race even a valid construct? This is a topic for many to discuss, but not a topic for this book. The term race is being used in this book for two reasons. It is used in all districts, all states, and at the national level for separating the students into groups. There is disproportionality across some groups and not others and the patterns of disproportionality are consistent. This is the problem. Yet this construct, valid or not, helps you know where to focus your efforts, once you know your numbers.

One more related note is the discussion of cultural competency versus cultural responsiveness. As noted earlier, Steve usually uses Latino and Black. Someone asked Steve why he was doing this, questioning his cultural competence. This question led Steve to add discussion on this topic to all of his 1-day trainings. In education, there has been a great effort to make people culturally competent, which is something Steve and others question. The concept of cultural competence is based on a belief that we can look at someone and tell by their appearance what culture they identify with and then apply our knowledge of that culture. Steve uses the word Latino, given that his Spanish teacher uses the term Latino. However, he has talked to many people who could be Latina, Hispanic, Cubano, Peruana, Chicano, etc about this very topic. Roughly 40% of the people Steve talked to identified as Hispanic and 40% Latino, with 20% not identifying as either, but instead as Cubano, Peruana, Chicano, etc. Also, Steve uses Black instead of African American, because two of his sons identify as Black, and not African American. Steve knows this because he asked them, independently, and they explained why they identify as Black and not African American. Steve also asked a co-worker the same question, and she identified as African American and explained why.

The point of this discussion is that we cannot know the cultural identity of someone by simply looking at them. Furthermore, even if we could, there are at least 400+ cultures within our schools (we have over 400 languages in our schools and that translates into well over 400 cultures), and we could not possibly know specific details about every one of these groups (even if we could identify people by their appearance). Instead, we need to be culturally responsive. We need to be careful in watching the people we work with. We need to watch their body language, have the courage to tell people that we need their help in understanding their culture, and have the courage to tell people that we might make mistakes and that we want them to educate us.

Did this chapter on Belief Systems and Acculturation change the way you look at the following chart?

A snapshot of one district's data…. Percentage ELL qualified for special education by building

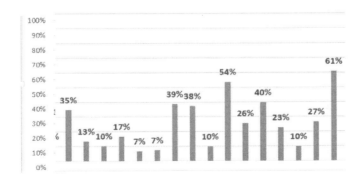

Do you now see that it is likely that the results are based upon inappropriate qualifications? Can you see yourself as part of the solution?

10. Qualification Does Not Equal Disability

Much research has been completed that helps to show that the rate in which we qualify students for special education is far above the rate that there are actually students with disabilities. Here are some examples:

First, the research completed by Steve showed that districts with low qualfications rates had low F/R meal rates and districts with high qualification rates had high F/R meal rates, and there is no relationship that is meaningful between poverty and disability rates for our students.

The research by Steve Hirsch and the research by Walter Gilliam help us to see that our biases are impacting our work, making many of our decisions very subjective instead of objective, and impacting our results.

Other research shows profoundly different rates of qualification for our children of color, depending upon where they live. You cannot have a disability that appears and disappears depending upon your zip code.

Research also shows the dramatically different qualification rates for our language learners depending upon whether or not there is a systematic tiered intervention system. In other words, if we meet their needs in general education we do not over qualify them for special education.

The rate of qualification for a specific learning disability tripled from the 1970's (far exceeding impact from population growth), leveled off between 2000 and 2004, and has been dropping since 2004. This has occured while RTI/MTSS has increased.

The state of Washington is one of the last states to implement a state supported RTI/MTSS initiative. Washington is one of the few states whose special education qualificition rate is increasing. It has increased almost every year since 2004. Interestingly enough, the trend line of this increase is very similar to the trend line of the increase of Latino students and ELL qualification.

Last, Ohio pays school districts for students who recieve special education services based upon the category of special education they qualify under. Is it a coincidence that two of the categories that are farthest above the national average for qualification rate are in the highest payment group? And the category that is the farthest below the national average for qualification rate is in the lowest payment group?

All of these things simply cannot be happening by chance!

"Takeaways"

1) We See What We are Acculturated to See: Real world examples of acculturation creating a lens. **We each need to examine the impact of our acculturation on our belief systems, on our practices, on our results.**

2) Steve's Personal Educator Journey: Real world example of developing over time, gaining new knowledge, and changing practices. **Self-examination can be painful, but we need to figure out what we don't know, combine that with our acculturation, and remain lifelong learners, painful as it will be at times.**

3) Steve Hirsh's and Walter Gilliam's Research: Research that shows the impact of our biases. **We all have biases, we need to examine how they are impacting our work, and our results.**

4) Monolingual Nation: Real world examples that help us see what could be unrealistic expectations and/or a lack of reasonable expectations. **We expect our students, at times, to achieve very difficult tasks. Can we prove that we are creating structures that lead to good results for the vast majority of our students??? A student is not necessarily disabled if they are struggling in a system in which more than 20% of the students are struggling!!!**

5) Literacy and Intelligence: Knowledge to help us see things differently. **We need to have knowledge to determine how things are related and correlated. Without this, we can make judgments that have no validity.**

6) Poverty: Research that shows our results, and indicates biases. **This is more evidence that our biases, beliefs, and acculturation impact our results. The more we know about where our problems are, the better we can focus on fixing our problems.**

7) Qualification vs Disability: Research that shows our results do not follow logical patterns, nor our "spoken" beliefs. **We need to examine our results and the results in our district, in order to understand where to begin our introspection, and where and how to change our practices.**

8) Reading and Referrals: Research that indicates our system, results, and beliefs have significant flaws. **There are methods out there that lead to different results. This shows us that many of the students we believe have disabilities are just not getting their needs met. What are we going to do?**

9) Race vs Disability: Research that shows our results, again, do not follow logical patterns, nor our "spoken" beliefs. **Again, our results do not match what we say that we believe. We need to examine our acculturation, belief systems and practices to achieve better results. No shame, no blame.**

10) Qualification Does Not Equal Disability. **We need to look at what we are doing. If our schools have a high rate of qualification, it is likely that we are putting students into special education who do not truly have disabilities, and this makes it more difficult for special education to have positive results. This does not mean they don't need help, just that special education is not the correct intervention.**

Closing Thoughts on Belief Systems

How do you change what people believe? As educators, we are caring individuals and lifelong learners. The problems, or poor results, within disproportionality are not occurring due to individuals purposefully doing harmful things to children. As educators see the impact of their actions or inactions in this area they will be highly motivated to change the results. Working on belief systems and acculturation, although painful at times, will be something that they do. Knowing that belief systems are a combination of acculturation and knowledge, educators will look for the knowledge they need (some of which can be found in Steve's and Ushani's books) and other information contained in the books of the many individuals we refer to within our books. Then, you can use the processes within Steve's and Ushani's books to change practices, which lead to changes in results.

Beliefs are very powerful; the following example comes from John Hattie's work.

John Hattie is possibly the leading expert in the world on what is and is not effective within educational strategies (Hattie's books, like Visible Learning, are powerful and useful books to own). An effect size of .4 is basically what is expected, the .9 is a very large effect size, and the 1.57 and 1.62 are extremely large effect sizes. The following are some examples found within his books or through Google searches:

-.34 for Mobility

-.02 for Summer Vacation

.19 for Co/Team Teaching

.47 for Small Group Learning

.53 for Scaffolding

.90 for Teacher Credibility

1.57 for Collective Teacher Belief

1.62 for Teacher Expectations of Student Performance

It is easy to see from this that beliefs have extremely powerful effects on our results. Also, having the knowledge, like that provided by Hattie, can sure save a lot of time, time that could be wasted on practices that are proven to have low impact on student learning.

Anthony Muhammad, author of several books, wrote the following in his book *Overcoming the Achievement Gap Trap*, "We cannot solve the problem until we look at it differently" (page 61) and "We cannot pursue equality when our value systems favor one group over another, especially when we lack the courage to even discuss the problem objectively" (page 75).

The work by Carol Dweck and her book on growth mindset versus fixed mindset is fantastic information for anyone in the process of evaluating and working on their own beliefs. It is also a great book for book study groups and the valuable discussions that can occur during book studies.

You have seen the problems, the issues about acculturation and belief systems, their impact on practice and results. It will take courage and knowledge to move forward. The good news is that better results lead to higher levels of satisfaction, so it will be worth it.

Chapter 3: Data Analysis

One of the goals of this work, in helping people to process their belief systems (and our own), is answering the question: Are you part of creating, sustaining, or solving the problem? Whatever the problem might be, we all fall into one of these three categories. People want to believe and/or have the perception that they are part of solving the problem, when they have no evidence to support that claim. In order to be part of solving the problem, one must know what the problem is, how big the problem is, and have taken action to make a difference in solving the problem. Therefore, if you don't know the data of your school, your district, your state in this area, it is highly unlikely that you are part of the solution and it is more likely that you are part of the creation or maintenance of the problem. This is not a criticism, but instead a perspective on this area that comes from working with thousands of people, across hundreds of districts, across many states, over a long period of time. So, part of the solution is getting data, yet you need to know what to look for in the data, where to start.

In working with school districts, Steve has experienced that roughly 50% of the districts can produce their own data correctly, meaning roughly 50% cannot produce their own data. There are times in which columns that should naturally add up to 100% are not even close. There are times in which a district reports more kids in a subgroup than in the group as a whole (e.g., more students who are dually qualified ELL/Special Education than the district has ELL qualified students), and there are times in which the data just doesn't make any sense at all (e.g., a category of eligibility being 20-50 times the national average for that category). Then, there are districts that literally state, "Sorry, but we cannot get you that data." Please note, the data being requested is, in general, data that is reported to the state for the state report cards or for the state grants. So, how do they get that data to report it to the state??? Some of these districts have admitted to "estimating" their data for state reports. An OSEP report from a few years ago had a sentence that roughly stated that they are unsure of the accuracy of their data, given so many states supply incorrect data. If your district is struggling at first to calculate their own data, this is not uncommon. Start wherever your district is, and grow from there.

The following pages include a series of questions that help districts look into their data. It is critical that, during this process, there is no blame and no shame. The data is a starting point for discussions and problem solving. The problems that exist didn't appear overnight and will not disappear overnight. So, get your data, examine your practices, take action, and repeat!

Do You Know Your School and District Data?

In order for a school to be able to say a student is not making reasonable progress, they need to know (not think) that their system is working and that their work is leading to proportional results. In order to do this, the school (and hopefully the district) needs to analyze their own data.

To start, you will need to answer this first set of questions that are related to the "big picture." Later we will provide a list of additional questions that require specific data to help provide answers. Researching the answers to these questions will lead to the systems level and building level analysis needed to understand the nature and location of the problems, the fine details.

- How do you know that your ELL students as a group are making progress? This is about how ELL students compare to other ELL students, as like as possible, and then across language groups. In order to answer this, you should know the growth rates of your students on the state language acquisition tests as compared to other ELL students in schools in your district, around your state and in the research. Also, your state department might have data that compares all of the school districts on some commonly measured areas (if they don't, ask them to create it).
- If you cannot prove average to above-average rates of growth, how do you know the student in question is not actually a curriculum or instructional casualty?
- What are the graduation rates of cohorts of ELL students, and how do they compare to non-ELLs?
- What are the graduation rates of ELL/Sped students, and how do they compare to other groups of students?
- For your ELL students, is there any difference in graduation rate by language spoken?

Understanding these problems often requires looking at these problems from a variety of angles. More questions, taken from a slightly different perspective:

- How do you know that your ELL students are progressing compared to non-ELL students? In order to answer this, you should know how your ELL students are doing on state and national testing as compared to non-ELL students.
- What are the demographics of the students who are qualified for special education services in your school and district? There are many questions to explore in this area. For example, if you have 20% of your students qualified for ELL services, are there only 20% of your special education students who are also ELL students (or less, given how hard it is to accurately qualify ELLs for SLD)? Are each of the languages proportionally represented within your special education student group? Are the disability categories being used at the same rates for your ELL/special education students as your non-ELL special education students?

How to Analyze School and District Data to Help Make Better Decisions

The short answer: easy, get all of the data and start asking and answering questions. The long answer is to start on the surface and keep digging deeper, asking more questions, as the following steps are going to delve into. The following questions and answers are examples and not all encompassing. Hopefully this will get teams off to a good start and then their individual circumstances will lead them to ask other questions.

1) What percentage of your district population is qualified for special education services?
2) How does that compare to the state average?
3) How does that compare to the national average?
4) How does that compare to districts with strong Response to Intervention (RTI) and/or Multi-Tiered Systems of Support (MTSS) models in your area?

5) Does your district have a strong RTI and/or MTSS Model?

Then, what about your ELL qualified students?

6) What percentage of your district is ELL qualified?
7) Of your students qualified for special education services, what percentage is also qualified for ELL services (or dually qualified students)?
8) Is the answer to number 7 slightly smaller than the answer to number 6? If not, there is a problem.

The questions numbers 6-8 focus on the special education population and on which students are also qualified for ELL services. The problem occurs when you have a higher percentage of students who are dually qualified than the percentage of students who are ELL qualified within your district. That is, if your district has 12% of the student population qualified for special education services and your district is 10% ELL qualified, yet 30% of the students in the special education population are ELL qualified students, you have a problem with over representation.

Another way to look at this:

9) What percentage of the ELL qualified student group is qualified for special education services? For example, if the overall percentage is 12% then the qualification rate within the ELL student group should be slightly lower.

Question number 9 looks at the ELL qualified population and which students are also qualified for special education services. The reason why the authors keep stating "slightly lower" is that qualifying a language learner as a student with a disability is a difficult task, if done accurately, so the rate should be slightly lower to equal. **You should graph this for all of your elementary schools and examine the differences.** It is less useful at secondary schools given that the majority of special education qualifications occur at the elementary school level. One caution regarding secondary students is the choice to qualify language learners for special education in order to utilize a different graduation standard, which is not appropriate (given the purpose and the likely lack of a disability, adverse impact and need for special education).

The next level of depth:

10) What is the percentage by race and by language spoken for each of the racial groups and each of the language groups within your district? Do you have a large number of groups yet some have very low representation? Depending upon your situation, you might want to calculate your percentages by language data for just your largest groups (e.g., the groups that add up to 90+% of your ELLs). Then, you can group the remaining language groups together or examine them separately, depending upon your district's issues.
11) What is the percentage each race and language group is represented within your special education qualified group?
12) What is the percentage each race and language is represented within your dually qualified group?

For number 11, the answers should match number 10. For number 12, you will need to subtract the native English speakers, and in some places the formerly ELLs, when examining the numbers.

13) What is the percentage, by language spoken, for each of the language groups within your district? Are there any tendencies by building?
14) What are the percentages, by language spoken, for your dually qualified students? Do this overall and by disability.
15) For all students qualified for special education, what is the percentage in each of the disability categories?
16) What is the percentage by language group and/or race represented within your special education qualified group by disability category?
17) Do the numbers appear logical or not? The percentages/proportions should be roughly equal (e.g., 17% of all students are language learners and 17% of the students qualified for special education are language learners, or anywhere between 16-18%).
18) How do your district's numbers compare to state and national numbers (found on the state report cards and the OSEP website, respectively)? Sometimes a request must be made, but this is public information.

   Given that there will be year-to-year variations, and results may be better or worse, trend lines must be positively related to the end goal. Trend data can also be helpful when examining small sample size groups. If there are significant differences, teams need to get together and have real conversations regarding why the differences exist and what the possible solutions are for the disproportionalities. No race, ethnic, nor language group has inherently higher rates of disabilities (qualification rates do not equal disability rates).

19) Does the distribution make sense based upon data? Within a building: Be careful with small data sets.

Another level:

20) What is the number of dually qualified students by school building?
21) For number 20, do those percentages match up with the ELL percentages in those buildings? For example, the building has 500 students, 20% of the students are ELL qualified (100 students) and the district has a 12% special education qualification rate and there are 12 dually qualified students (12% of 100). Or, there are 24 dually qualified students, and the numbers do not make sense!
22) What is your percentage of ELL students qualified for special education by elementary building (make a graph)? Of your ELL qualified students, what percentage are special education qualified (e.g., if there are 30 ELL students in the building and 15 are special education qualified, the percentage is 50%)?

Within each building:

23) Do the categories of qualification match the percentages at the district level? In other words, if SLD is used 37% of the time across the district, is each building using SLD 37% of the time with their dually qualified students?
24) Within each building are there specific problems related to any of the disability categories?
25) Within each building are there specific problems related to any of the racial groups?
26) Within each building are there specific problems related to any of the linguistic groups?
27) Are there any issues by evaluator? For example, if you had 41 buildings and 79% of the language learners qualified for Speech or Language Impairment existed in just 6 of your buildings, there could be a need to have conversations with the SLPs who serve these buildings. For example, if your building with the largest number of language learners qualified for special education were qualified under SLD at 80% of these students and they all spoke the same language (even though the building had 42 languages), then there would be a need to have a discussion with the school psychologist. These are real examples.

The first time this is done, for any major "problem area" an individual will need to examine the specific students (likely needing to examine the actual files) and answer the following:

28) What percentage of the students within that group were qualified within the district?
29) Of the students qualified within the district, which buildings were those students qualified in?
30) What was the date of the qualification for the problem area? Using this information, what was the student's language acquisition level at that time? Create a chart for this.

It is common that many of the students were qualified for SLD (often Speech or Language Impaired and Developmentally Delayed, too) while they were at language acquisition level 1 and there is no data to support the problem existed in their native language.

31) What percentage of your district is qualified for F/R meals?
32) What percentage of your special education qualified students are also qualified for F/R meals?
33) How do the results of these recent questions look? That is, is there proportionality or not?
34) Break down the results from above by building. Is there any correlation to ELL eligibility and/or F/R lunch percentages by building?
35) How does that compare to the state average? Your first goal is to at least be on the positive side of the state averages, knowing that the state averages might also be demonstrating systems level problems.

Your district will also need to examine the data for your students who have been qualified for ELL services for a period of time much longer than is the norm. Many states use the 5-year mark as a dividing line. Your state likely has data regarding the percentage of students "exited" from

ELL services within the first 5 years (your state might use 4 years or 6 years). The students who exceed this timeframe are often referred to as long-term English learners (LTELs).

36) Are your LTELs primarily from your largest one or two language groups?
37) How large is your LTEL group?
38) Is your district doing anything different in an attempt to prevent this from occurring?
39) Have you factored these answers into your special education evaluation? In other words, if you have a large LTEL group and the student of concern comes from this group, how do you figure out whether or not their real problem is that they are a system, instructional, and/or curriculum casualty?

For Smaller Schools and Smaller Districts (Small Sample Sizes):

In these cases, you might need to look at historical data in order to build a data set that covers several years of time. That is, look at patterns over time in order to make sure that small sample sizes are not leading to incorrect assumptions, either positive or negative. Also, in smaller schools and districts, the teams might need to examine each and every case in an effort to best understand what is occurring. For example, if your district has 300 students, 30 of which are language learners, and 10 are qualified for special education, your data will look very bad. It is possible that each of those 10 students truly is a student with a disability. It is also possible that your system is not working well and you are over qualifying students. Your teams will need to look at each of these evaluations and the services these students are receiving for language acquisition. Have the tough discussions, with no shame and no blame. Seek to understand. Then, modify your system as needed to make sure each of these students is getting their needs met, whether within or outside special education.

In General:

Once you know the patterns for your school and your district and you have compared them to state and national data, introspection is crucial. If your building (and district) has clear issues with over qualification by race, language, ethnicity, etcetera, how will you be able to factor that into your decision-making process? Please note, most schools and districts currently do have problems in these areas, so it is critical that staff do not lose hope or become overly critical once these problems are identified. Instead, staff need to have real and open discussions on why these results are the way they are currently. In education, it is profoundly rare to find a staff member who is not a caring and loving individual (even if they try to play it otherwise). We are good people doing hard work. So, take these crucial and difficult conversations seriously, yet focus on solutions and not blame. Once a path toward achieving better results has been set forth, it will take 3-5 years to see large measurable change. Remember, no blame and no shame!

The data regarding proportional or disproportional distribution within special education is something that should be known prior to starting the matrix process. For example, if you did not know that only 60% of the students in your school, or your district, are successful with the core instruction, you would not know that the student you are examining could be a casualty of a system that is not working for students in general. If you did not know that your district is qualifying Black/African American students as intellectually disabled at twice the rate of the state, you would not know to go the extra mile when evaluating a student who is Black/African American to ensure accuracy. If you did not know that your district uses the category of Specific Learning Disability for all students in special education at a rate of 37%, but uses it at 70% for the ELL/special education dually qualified students, you would not know there was a problem in that area. If you did not know that 100% of your dually qualified students all speak the same language, and you have 22 languages in your district, you would not know there is a problem. Examining your data helps to ensure that you are not part of creating or maintaining the problem, instead you have the opportunity to be part of solving the problem. These are real life examples and not even the most extreme examples.

In order for a school to be able to say a student is not making reasonable progress, they need to know (not think) that their system is working for the vast majority of students and that their work is leading to proportional results.

Chapter 4: LE³AP

LE³AP

Look at:

Exposure

Experience

Expectations

and

Practice

The LE³AP process takes into account these four main areas, in order to understand whether the skill deficit in question is related to Exposure, Experience, Expectations, and Practice versus a possible disability. In other words, once a team has looked at a problem with the "lens" of exposure, experience, expectations and practice, does the presenting problem appear (all things considered) reasonable or does it appear to represent a potential disability?

These four areas are being differentiated as follows:

Exposure: The team looks at whether or not the student was exposed to the area of concern in a manner similar to students who have learned the skill/behavior in question.

Experience: Is differentiated by looking at whether or not the student was actively involved in the skill/behavior similar to students who developed the skill/behavior in question.

Expectation(s): Did the adults in the student's environment expect them to attempt/learn the new skill/behavior? How did they support that learning? And how do those expectations and support compare with what you would normally see for a child who has learned that skill/behavior?

Practice: Examines what the student (or adults) did in order for the student to get better at the skill/behavior and how that compares to students who have acquired the skill/behavior in question. Practice is a focused effort on improving a skill, not solely active participation in the skill/activity (e.g., working on phoneme skills development versus pleasure reading). Practice can be equated to intervention in many cases.

It is important to note that some students do not have exposure and/or experience given that they have a disability that limited their exposure and/or experience. For a student who clearly has a medical condition that impacts their access to their education or for a student who clearly has a cognitive impairment (referring to students who are likely to have intelligence test scores in the 50-60 or lower range), a process like this should be abbreviated as appropriate (based upon the documented evidence). In this case, the process might become more about data gathering for the referral and potential evaluation process (based upon facts, not impressions).

The following five examples provide some context.

Student 1:

This student was a 6th grade student who was performing well below grade level expectations. He is from a Russian background and he is one of many siblings. The majority of his siblings were doing well in school, yet a few were doing poorly. All indicators were leading toward a special education referral. The school psychologist was in the process of interviewing the student's mother, and the information continued to support the possibility of a special education referral. Then, his mother stated, "You know he can read and write in Russian, right?" This information was not known to the team, so the school psychologist asked if they could use the interpreter to get an example of her son's reading and writing skills in Russian.

The student came into the school psychologist's office and the school psychologist opened a webpage in Russian, asking the student to read the information and provide a summary. The student did this and provided a detailed summary, and the interpreter stated that the summary was accurate. Then, the school psychologist wrote questions in English that the interpreter did not get to see. The student wrote responses to the questions in Russian and the interpreter read these. She stated that the written responses were easy to understand, just with some misspellings. The school psychologist asked the student's mother about the family's emphasis on English versus Russian. The student had 1 hour per week of class in Russian. The mother made it clear that it is very important to the family that the student learns to read and write in Russian, and that it is not so important that he reads and writes in English. They have a family business in which all of the boys are expected to work, and they need to be able to speak, read, and write in Russian for the business.

Exposure: The student has been exposed to English since very early in his life.

Experience: The student has been in an English school since Kindergarten, and was participating at a low level.

Expectations: The family expects Russian skills to be learned and mastered, not English skills.

Practice: The student had a long history of completing very little work within the school setting.

Knowing all of this, is it really reasonable to expect him to have grade level skills in English???

And, a student who can read/write in their native language at a higher level than in English (with far less exposure and experience) is not a student with a learning disability.

Student 2:

A little boy or girl, 3 to 4 years of age is having a very difficult time pronouncing their words, and does not appear to even be trying. When this child wants some cereal, their mom or dad or older sibling goes to the cupboard because the child is pointing that direction and grunting. Then, they open the cupboard and the adult (or older sibling) points to the first box. The child says, "untuh." The adult or older sibling points to the second box. The child says, "untuh." Then the third box, and the child responds, "unhuh." The adult or older sibling then pulls this box down, fills a bowl with cereal and gives it to the child. The child has had their needs met without using appropriate language skills.

Exposure: It is highly likely that the child has heard all of the correct words.

Experience: The child has not been using or attempting to use the correct words.

Expectations: The adults are not expecting the child to use or attempt to use the correct words.

Practice: The child is not practicing the needed skills, whether approximations that could be shaped or the actual words.

This child could be a child with a disability or non-disability developmental delay, yet it would be very difficult to accurately assess this skill set, not knowing what some intervention and work with the family could achieve.

Student 3:

A fourth-grade boy was having a very difficult time with reading comprehension. His entire family (other than his siblings) spoke zero English and his family stayed within the Latino community to get all of their needs met. His parents are literate in Spanish, but had told him that they didn't want him learning to read in Spanish until after he had learned to read in English without problems. The team talked with the parents and the parents agreed to allow the school psychologist, who happens to read in Spanish, to work with him on Spanish reading skills. In about 6 weeks the boy was reading with comprehension, with most of the teaching regarding letter sounds. He then was able to comprehend at a higher level in Spanish than in English. It turned out that his basic language skills (i.e., BICS) were primarily in Spanish and his academic language skills (i.e., CALP) were primarily in English. It was very difficult for him to use contextual clues while reading in English, given he was missing many of the words. Yet, in Spanish he knew the words and could use them to figure out the more difficult words using contextual clues.

Exposure: He was exposed to the English words.

Experience: He did not use his English skills much, given he had no use for them outside of school. Within the school setting, there are many words that one is unlikely or less likely to use.

Expectations: Parents expected him to learn in English before developing the skill in Spanish.

Practice: There was no practice that was addressing the core problem, given that the core problem was not known.

This student benefitted greatly from the intervention that was focused on his actual need. This "practice" allowed him the opportunity to understand how to use contextual clues, using his stronger language. Then, he was able to transfer this skill into his work in English.

Student 4:

This student was also a fourth-grade student, and actually happened to be in the same classroom as student number 3. This student was having a very specific problem, he was struggling greatly with phonics and phonemes when reading. His parents were reading to him in Spanish and trying to work with him on these issues. His little sister (same environment as him) was in the second grade and already reading at a higher level than this student. Also, his parents were the only people in his world who spoke Spanish 100% of the time, his other relatives usually spoke English.

Exposure: He had been exposed to reading in English and had multiple years of intervention for the problems/concerns he was demonstrating.

Experience: He was trying to read in English and in Spanish, with support in both languages.

Expectations: His parents and school staff all had high expectations of him. His writing was at grade level if spelling was not taken into account, his math calculations were at grade level independently, and his math problem solving was at grade level when the problems were read to him.

Practice: He had had several years of intervention that was designed to target his problems with phonics and phonemes.

This student was referred for a special education evaluation. His problem was very specific in nature and was showing up across both languages. He had been exposed to the skill that he was not developing, he had experience with these skills, he was expected to learn these skills, and he was given an intervention (practice) designed to improve these skills. These facts, along with the fact that his sister (same environment, two years younger) was reading at a higher-grade level than him, were all factors that helped determine that he was a student in need of special education services.

Student 5:

Soon after arriving in the United States, a parent came into the school and made a special education referral for her son prior to his first day of school. The school psychologist visited with her and talked about how unusual that was, explaining that we normally allow the student to start school, that we try to get to know the student, and then determine an appropriate action plan. She explained, through an interpreter she had brought with her, that her son had autism and was severely impacted. She had a stack of medical records and reports (all translated into English), and she wanted a special education evaluation. The school psychologist asked her to bring him to school later that day, to get an opportunity to meet him. She was very hesitant, believing that this was a very bad idea. She did bring him into the school later that day, and the school psychologist observed that he was, indeed, extremely impacted due to his autism.

Exposure: This child had had very little exposure to school and to his new environment.

Experience: This child had had no experience with a school in the new environment.

Expectations: He was expected to behave appropriately and to attempt to learn, but at this time the impact of his autism limited his success greatly.

Practice: There was very little practice that was occurring, given it was very difficult to obtain and maintain his attention on the wanted behaviors.

This student did not have the exposure, experience, nor practice. However, he was severely impacted by his disability and the fact that he did not speak English was not the determining factor in this situation. He was qualified for special education services within 10 school days.

Summary:

These examples provide a glimpse into using the LE^{3}AP process. This framework is meant to help staff look at problems based upon examining what is reasonable or likely, given exposure/experience/expectations/practice. Also, these steps provide information that helps staff reason through the design of potential interventions, or develop reasoning for the referral process, and/or develop reasoning and data for the evaluation process. Last, the final example demonstrates that, at times, the disability is the determining factor and not the lack of English language development.

Chapter 5: Systematic Approach to the Problems

Introduction

The ELL Critical Data Process began as a graduate level project for Steve when he was studying language acquisition. At the time, Steve was working in the Kent School District, and they wanted him to have a known expert in the field provide input into whether or not the process appeared to have validity. The expert told many people that the work was ground breaking in the field. From that moment forward, Steve has been working extensively on the process, training on the process, and writing books related to the process.

After about six years of training and working on the process, Steve and Ushani re-wrote their first book, the book that centers on the ELL Critical Data Process. The re-write was based upon what was learned during that period of time from working with and training thousands of educators on the process.

During the re-write of the first book, Steve added an addendum that focused on how to utilize the data from the ELL Critical Data process to assist in understanding whether or not a language learner who is struggling is a language learner who also happens to have a Specific Learning Disability. This is the most difficult area to do correctly, yet has the most disproportionality of any of the special education eligibility categories for our language learners, and is the largest category of eligibility by a wide margin. This chapter discusses using the ELL Critical Data Process data to assist in making that determination. You will find information on all disability categories in Chapter 8 and Appendix A.

Some of the appendices of this book provide additional information on special education categories in general, and also for the category of specific learning disability.

The ELL Critical Data Process

The ELL Critical Data Process was created to provide staff with a systematic methodology to help understand which students are reasonable candidates for a special education referral and which candidates really should receive more targeted intervention in place of considering a special education referral.

The process helps the staff analyze 16 key points of data and chart the meaning of each piece of data so that the end result is a visual representation (the matrix) of their discussions. Also, throughout these discussions the team will learn what is adversely impacting the student's education, so that they can design and implement appropriate interventions (if that has not already occurred or if the results are not strong enough). In virtually all cases, staff believe that they have provided appropriate interventions. A trainer trained in this process can help staff see that, without research and data to back them up, they really do need to rethink their approach. A prime example of this is the methodology used for delivery of ELL services. If you have not already read and studied the work by Dr. Thomas and Dr. Collier on this, you will find it very helpful. The most widely used teaching method for ELL students is the "pull-out" model, and research shows this model is not only ineffective, but may be harmful. And, it is the most expensive model. So, why are we doing it? There are some reasons that are rational for using this method, yet we need to shift and adjust based upon the research and common sense. In consulting with many districts, there appears to be a widespread movement toward push-in ELL services (potentially in response to the research). However, in many cases it became clear during consultation, that the push-in services were being provided by individuals with no training in language acquisition and/or without an overarching plan on how the services would be directly linked to the commonly accepted language acquisition standards. In these districts, the initial results appear to indicate the students are performing very poorly after receiving services that are not meeting their needs, which should not surprise anyone. Knowledge, based upon data, regarding the effectiveness of the ELL services model in your district is crucial knowledge and part of using the ELL Critical Data Process.

Once the staff have been trained on and have used the Critical Data Process, they have an opportunity to see more possibilities. The Preschool model focuses primarily on exposure, expectations, experience and practice, given there is less measurable data available. The K-12 model looks at exposure and experience, and then adds areas in which measurable data is available.

For the purposes of this discussion, we are going to assume a team has followed the process with fidelity and has concluded that a special education referral is the appropriate action. At this time, the team has data that indicates that the student is not learning at the same rate as his/her peers and is not responding to interventions like his/her peers, and there is no other reason for the problems that should be intervened upon prior to moving forward (e.g., impact of trauma).

The like peer group provides stronger data the more the peers are like the student of concern regarding language spoken, time in the US, type of ELL services provided, etcetera. However, there will be times in which finding like peers is very difficult. For "rare" students, meaning there are no other students who speak the same language within the setting, these students tend to be less commonly referred and/or qualified (there is less disproportionality data within these groups), the team just needs to find other students who are less common linguistically, but match for other factors like time learning English. Do not use students from commonly found linguistic groups within your district as comparison students for the less commonly found linguistic groups. Then, if you are in a very small district, work with your agency (e.g., ESD or AEA) to find like peers.

But, any time we make an assumption we take a very large risk.

Let's pause and make sure that you (your team, school, and district) have done the homework needed to be on reasonably safe ground. Let's take the guess work out of this.

First, you have collected and analyzed your district data. If problems with disproportionality exist your teams have increased the intentionality and intensity of using the ELL Critical Data Process and targeted intervention, and the data is still saying to move forward. And, you have examined the situation using the LE^{3}AP lens. Or, you are talking about a student who is likely to have a disability in a category that does not have disproportionality (see chapter 8 for information on this), like students with blindness or deafness.

Now, if you are looking at the most difficult category to do well, Specific Learning Disability, the following pages help you to integrate the data from the ELL Critical Data Process with your evaluation data to increase the likelihood of an accurate result.

Specific Learning Disability and ELL Students with less than 5 years learning English

The descriptions below show how the data for these items can support eligibility for special education services, be neutral on the issue, or contradict eligibility for special education services. If the team has parent permission to evaluate a language learner and there is a possibility of a specific learning disability, these items and this information needs to be carefully considered and documented.

Please note, this information is not as useful if the team does not know their data on their usage of SLD as a category for all students versus language learners and do not know the success rate of ELL students within the school and district (e.g., rates of language acquisition, test scores on local, state and national tests, graduation rates).

Your decision making gets stronger if your data proves that you have a system in which language learners are not overqualified in general and are having success in general (based upon data/proof) and your decision making gets weaker as your data shows over qualification and/or poor performance of ELL students in general (poor language acquisition, poor general test scores). In other words, strong performance in general of the ELLs and a student who is doing very poorly indicates an individual student problem. In contrast, poor performance of students in general makes it near impossible to separate ELLs with disabilities from students who are casualties of a system that does not work well for students in general.

There are more items below regarding supporting eligibility given that most students who are considered for a special education referral should not reach the stage of a special education evaluation unless there is already supporting data that a special education evaluation is needed.

Names of the items, by number, from the ELL Critical Data Process

Not all items are included in the examples that follow, given that not all of the items load into the decision-making process for the possibility of a specific learning disability.

1. Student's Primary Language
2. Students who speak multiple languages
3. Language Confusion
4. **Red Flag Area**- Education in Primary/Native Language
5. Parental literacy in primary language
6. **Red Flag Area**- Student did not learn to read in the primary language
7. **Red Flag Area**- Years learning English

8. Attendance History
9. Approach taken with regards to ELL services
10. **Red Flag Area**- Rate of growth on the state language acquisition test
11. **Red Flag Area**- Intervention Description
12. Expectations in the general education classroom
13. Classroom observation
14. Comparison Student Data
15. **Red Flag Area**- The parent interview
16. Developmental History

Items and examples in which Specific Learning Disability is not supported by item:

Item 3: If the student of concern does not demonstrate language confusion while learning multiple languages, this is data indicating that they do not have a learning disability.

Item 4: If there is evidence of formal education in primary language and average to above average performance, this is data indicating that they do not have a learning disability.

Item 6: If the student of concern learned to read in their native language, this is data indicating that they do not have a learning disability.

Item 8: If the student of concern is not attending school in the US, because in their country they were successful in school and they are not successful here in the US, this is data indicating that they do not have a learning disability.

Item 10: If the student of concern is learning English at the same rate as their like peers, this is data indicating that they do not have a learning disability.

Item 11: If the student of concern responds positively to targeted intervention, at a level similar to or higher than like peers, this is data indicating that they do not have a learning disability.

Item 14: If there is another source of data used to compare the student of concern against like peers for rate of learning, and the student of concern scores in a similar manner to that of like peers, this is data indicating that they do not have a learning disability.

Item 15: If there is no past evidence of learning problems for the student of concern, nor within the family, this is data indicating that they do not have a learning disability.

Items and examples in which Specific Learning Disability is neutral by item:

Item 4: If there is evidence that the student of concern did poorly during education in their primary language, but the system is known to have inconsistent levels of success for students, then this evidence is neutral (does not help during the evaluation process).

Item 6: If the student of concern did not have a reasonable opportunity to learn to read in their native language, and didn't learn to read in their native language, then this evidence is neutral (does not help during the evaluation process).

Item 9: If the student of concern is receiving ELL services in a system that is not proven to have strong results, per the research or evidence, then this evidence is neutral (does not help during the evaluation process).

Item 11: If the student of concern is receiving a targeted intervention and their performance is only slightly lower than that of like peers, then this evidence is neutral (does not help during the evaluation process).

Item 12: If the student of concern is in a classroom or system in which the expectations for ELL students or specifically for this student are below average, then this evidence is neutral (does not help during the evaluation process).

Item 13: If the student of concern is not appearing engaged in the classroom, then this evidence is neutral (does not help during the evaluation process).

Item 14: If there is another source of data used to compare the student of concern against like peers for rate of learning, and the student of concern scores are slightly lower than those of like peers, then this evidence is neutral (does not help during the evaluation process).

Items and examples in which Specific Learning Disability is supported by item:

Item 3: If the student of concern is showing language confusion, has had a real opportunity to develop both languages to a usable/useful level (additional support would be siblings in same environment do not have language confusion), and they are over the age of 8, this becomes stronger and stronger evidence in support of a possible learning disability based upon how far they are above the age of 8, how well their siblings have done, and how strong the evidence is for simultaneous bilingual/multilingual environment.

Item 4: If there is evidence that the student of concern had formal education in their native language and they did poorly (when peers and/or siblings did well), then this is supportive data for the possibility of a learning disability (this becomes stronger as the student of concern is more unlike peers and/or siblings in the same environment).

Item 5: If the parents of the student of concern are highly literate in the commonly used language (language spoken between parents and child), and they read to the student of concern in this language, and this student is doing poorly in school, then this is evidence that supports the possibility of a learning disability.

Item 6: If the student of concern had a strong opportunity to learn to read in their native language (peers and/or siblings learned to read in the same environment), and the student of concern did not learn to read, then this is evidence that supports the possibility of a learning disability.

Item 8: If the student of concern is not attending school because they have a history of doing poorly in school (peers and/or siblings normally did well in the same environment), then this is evidence that supports the possibility of a learning disability.

Item 9: If the student of concern is in a dual language ELL service model, or an ELL service model in which the team can prove with data that their students in general are successful with the model used, and this student is not successful, then this is evidence that supports the possibility of a learning disability. This is stronger and stronger as the student is more unlike their language learning peers (i.e., if this is the only language learner having learning difficulties, this would be very strong data).

Item 10: If the student of concern is acquiring English at a much slower rate than their like peers in your school, based on state language acquisition testing, then this is evidence that supports the possibility of a learning disability.

Item 11: If the student of concern is responding to targeted intervention at a much slower rate than like peers, then this is evidence that supports the possibility of a learning disability.

Item 12: If the student of concern is in an environment in which there are strong expectations that are supported by a system of support (evidence is needed to prove this, not opinion), and the student is doing poorly, then this is evidence that supports the possibility of a learning disability.

Item 13: If the student of concern is in a well-run classroom, and they are engaged in the learning (using the evidence of watching peers and teachers then trying to mimic or copy what they are doing), and this student is producing very low-quality work (in comparison to like peers), and the quality is not improving, then this is evidence that supports the possibility of a learning disability.

Item 14: If the student of concern is shown to score much lower than like peers on measurable data, then this is evidence that supports the possibility of a learning disability.

Item 15: If the parents report that the student of concern has always struggled with learning (and/or have report cards from the previous environment) and those struggles match the struggles that the team is seeing in the current environment, then this is evidence that supports the possibility of a learning disability.

School Psychologists:

For each of these examples, you can take what is written above and make minor modifications to use within your evaluation report to address whether or not language learning or the disability is the determinant factor. The following are examples of this. And, you would need to do the same for each of the items in which there are meaningful results.

An example for using an item as one of the pieces of data within the report to indicate a student **is not** eligible for special education as a student with a learning disability:

Statement from above:

Item 11: If the student responds positively to targeted intervention, at or higher than like peers, this is data indicating that they do not have a learning disability.

What you could write:

Jose was involved in a targeted intervention to address concerns regarding his skills in reading vocabulary. This area was targeted for intervention given that he was found to be in the lowest 10% of the fourth-grade students in this area. When Jose was compared to like peers (other ELL students who speak Spanish and have been learning English for 3 years), his rate of growth during the intervention was within the average for the group. Therefore, this is evidence to indicate that Jose does not have a Specific Learning Disability.

An example for using an item as one of the pieces of data within the report to indicate a student **is** eligible for special education as a student with a learning disability:

Statement from above:

Item 11: If the student of concern is responding to targeted intervention at a much slower rate than like peers, then this is evidence that supports the possibility of a learning disability.

What you could write:

Jose was involved in a targeted intervention to address concerns regarding his skills in reading vocabulary. This area was targeted for intervention given that he was found to be in the lowest 10% of the fourth-grade students in this area. When Jose was compared to like peers (other ELL students who speak Spanish and have been learning English for 3 years), his rate of growth during the intervention was significantly lower than that of his peers. When this piece of data is combined with _____ (your other supporting data), this is evidence that learning English is not the determinant factor with regards to the delayed development Jose is demonstrating, but instead that Jose has a specific learning disability. The combination of the evidence indicates that Jose would demonstrate this disability regardless of whether or not he was a language learner.

Analysis matrix for suspicion of SLD in language learners with less than 5 years learning English

FACTORS	3	4	5	6	8	9	10	11	12	13	14	15
Data supports SLD qualification												
Neutral												
Data does not support SLD qualification												
	3	4	5	6	8	9	10	11	12	13	14	15

The matrix you will be working with when completing the ELL Critical Data Process will have the red-flag areas highlighted in red and the neutral row highlighted in green. In order to reduce the cost printing this book we are providing you the matrix without the color coding. Also, this matrix does not use all of the factors/numbers, because not all of the numbers provide information regarding SLD for language learners with less than 5 years learning English.

Are there mostly marks in "neutral" and "Data supports SLD qualification?" Then the evidence is likely to be supportive of a special education qualification, knowing the work has been completed across the ELL Critical Data Process, school/district data analysis, and the special education evaluation.

Any marks in the "Data does not support SLD qualification" section should be carefully examined and discussed before moving forward. Anything that brings into question the decision to qualify a language learner as a student with a specific learning disability must be examined and explained so that a stranger to the student can understand what decision was made, what data the decision was based upon, and that the decision appears logical given the data. **Important: This is in addition to meeting your district and state expectations, and in addition to the Face Validity described in Appendix A.**

Chapter 6: Examples for Special Education Evaluation Reports

This chapter focuses on giving example wording that can be used within special education evaluation reports. The examples are listed first by disability category and then by ELL Critical Data Process item number. The examples by disability category focus more on statements about issues that relate to reliability, validity, and adverse impact as related to the disability. The categories without as many issues regarding disproportionality (primarily those other than SLD, SLI and DD) have less variance, and the categories of SLD, SLI and DD have much more variation in information and examples provided.

The CFRs use "adverse impact" in the majority of the disability categories, but for unknown reasons not all of the categories. Some states, like Washington, have put that wording into all of the eligibility categories. The examples in the first section include the wording of adverse impact. Confusion occurs with staff around the *concept* of "adverse impact" and the *words* adverse impact. The concept "adverse impact" is about how a disability is creating an adverse impact on the child's ability to access their education and that requires special education services. The confusion is that these children are doing poorly in school. Therefore, staff relate the words adverse impact to doing poorly in school. However, the doing poorly in school could be related to many other issues discussed in this book and could have no relationship to a disability.

The examples that focus on item numbers from the ELL Critical Data Process are examples that focus on data that either supports or does not support the likelihood of a student being eligible for special education services.

The like peer group provides stronger data the more the peers are like the student of concern regarding language spoken, time in the US, type of ELL services provided, etcetera. However, there will be times in which finding like peers is very difficult. For "rare" students, meaning there are no other students who speak the same language within the setting, these students tend to be less commonly referred and/or qualified (there is less disproportionality data within these groups), the team just needs to find other students who are less common linguistically, but match for other factors like time learning English. Do not use students from commonly found linguistic groups within your district as comparison students for the less commonly found linguistic groups. Then, if you are in a very small district, work with your agency (e.g., ESD or AEA) to find like peers.

Examples by Category of Disability (followed by examples by ELL Critical Data Process Item number)

Hearing Impairment

1) Documentation of impact of language on hearing testing (did the student fully understand the directions).

   Example: Impact was limited through the usage of interpreter, and the interpreter reported that the student understood the directions. Also, the observation of the student indicated that he or she responded without difficulty to the directions within the range of their previously demonstrated hearing.

2) For adverse impact, documentation of how language learning and hearing are each separately related to the adverse impact.

   Example: When testing in the area of communication, he or she was able to quickly and successfully respond to the practice items and easier items. When the items became more difficult, the student's answers were indicative of a lack of knowledge and not a lack of understanding (e.g., he or she gave an answer that is related logically, yet wrong).

Deafness

1) Documentation of impact of language on hearing testing (did the student fully understand the directions).

   Example: The impact was limited through the usage of a sign language interpreter (making sure it is the correct sign language), and the interpreter reported that the student understood the directions. Also, the observation of the student indicated that he or she responded without difficulty to the directions within the range of their previously demonstrated hearing (Deaf and Hard of Hearing and/or Hearing Impairment are sometimes combined within one eligibility category).

2) For adverse impact, documentation of how language learning and hearing are each separately related to the adverse impact.

   Example: When testing fine motor skills, and using a sign language interpreter who signs in the correct form, she or he demonstrated the ability to understand the practice items and easier items.

Visual Impairment-Blindness

1) Documentation of impact of language on vision testing (did the student fully understand the directions).

   Example: Impact was limited through the usage of an interpreter, and the interpreter reported that the student understood the directions. Also, the observation of the student indicated that he or she responded without difficulty to the directions within the range their previously demonstrated vision.

2) For adverse impact, documentation of how language learning and vision are each separately related to the adverse impact.

   Example: During the testing, she or he demonstrated the ability to perform tasks at a level that is similar to the level reported by the parent and a level that was within the expected range given the documentation of past performance levels.

Orthopedic Impairment

1) Documentation of impact of language on motor testing (did the student fully understand the directions).

   Example: Prior to the testing he or she was observed in a non-test environment. The physical skills demonstrated during the formal testing are similar to those previously observed, the expectations based upon the parent interview, and the documentation provided from the previous school.

2) For adverse impact, documentation of how language learning and physical restrictions created by the orthopedic issues are each separately related to the adverse impact.

   Example: During the assessment, the interpreter was able to explain the directions and check for understanding. The student confirmed with the interpreter that they understood the task, but explained that they could not do portions of the task (e.g., block design). Therefore, the team concluded that the non-motor tasks of the intellectual testing and the non-motor academic tasks are valid and reliable measures. In contrast, the motor involved tasks are reliable (meaning the scores would likely be similar each time) and not valid (given the test is not normed on individuals with motor impairments that are not related to intellectual ability or academic ability).

Traumatic Brain Injury (TBI)

1) Documentation of impact of language on all testing (did the student fully understand the directions).

   Example: The team has documented his or her performance on the areas evaluated prior to the injury. The current performance is notably lower in all areas. Therefore, the impact of limited English skills is not the primary factor.

2) For adverse impact, documentation of how language learning and the brain injury are each separately related to the adverse impact.

   Example: The team has documented the areas the student struggled in prior to the injury, and the extent of the struggles, as they were primarily related to the impact of the student being a language learner. The current evaluation documents the areas in which he or she is now having moderate to severely delayed performance, beyond what was previously noted.

   Important: The writer of the report needs to compare and contrast the documented differences to support or negate that the issues are more related to the TBI or more related to language acquisition.

Deaf-Blind

Important: Students who are both deaf and blind are very rare. Also, the likelihood of a student who is deaf and blind, language learner or not, needing special education support is virtually 100%. The fact that any given student is a language learner will add to their needs in general in a new culture and language.

Multiple Disabilities

Important: The student must meet the criteria of two or more of the other categories. A student who truly meets the criteria for Multiple Disabilities is a student whose individual disabilities are additively impacting them in a severe manner. It is unlikely that language learning would be anything other than an additional factor to provide support for during learning.

Autism

1) Documentation of impact of language on all testing (did the student fully understand the directions).

Important: 1) Students with Autism in general have difficulties with communication, especially pragmatic communication. This makes the testing even more complex. 2) These examples are primarily for Asperger's like students, or HFA like students.

Example: The team worked with the family to understand the impacts of the autism on communication in his or her native language. Then, the team, with the family, discussed how this might have factored into the academic, communication, and intellectual testing. The team determined that in the native language this only impacts him/her when the subject matter is abstract. Therefore, concrete subject matters like basic math skills and basic reading skills were not dually impacted by the autism and language learning, whereas math problem solving (understanding the word problems) and reading comprehension (understanding implications) are more impacted. The team is recommending services based on the data and the perceived impact.

2) For adverse impact, documentation of how language learning and the impacts of Autism are each separately related to the adverse impact.

Important: See above. Additionally, for the students whose autism impacts them on a more global and intense level, the team might write:

Example: The student's autism impacts all aspects of daily life. The parents have reported this through interview and this has been seen through observation. There are global developmental delays when he/she is functioning within groups who are solely communicating in his/her native language. Therefore, the impact of being a language learner is secondary to the impact of the autism.

3) Autism is in many ways a disability of "communication." The team needs to be able to describe the likely impact of the Autism versus the likely impact of the language learning. In other words, how would the student function (demonstrate adverse impact and need for SDI) if they were not a language learner?

Important: See the above statements and add additional commentary as needed. For example, the team might write the following:

Example: The parent interview and developmental history have documented the impacts of communication delays related to autism that are occurring within the native language of the student. For example, even within a group of peers speaking his/her language, he/she demonstrates a great deal of difficulty understanding the unspoken meaning or implications of the conversation and this, at times, leads to frustration and poor behavior that is solely based upon misunderstandings that are not related to or not primarily related to learning English.

Intellectual Disability (ID)

1) Documentation of impact of language on all testing (did the student fully understand the directions). The team needs to be able to show, with the integration of multiple sources of data, how language impacts the testing. Can the team clearly state that the scores would be in the ID range if the student was not a language learner?

   Example: Intellectual testing in the non-native language is problematic. The team has therefore taken the caution to examine supporting data in relationship to the student's intellectual testing score. He/she scored a standard score of 58 on the testing. This score is indicative of a student with significant intellectual processing difficulties. The adaptive behavior scores are commensurate with the documented intellectual ability score. Knowing that cultural issues can arise during adaptive behavior measurement, the team is using observational data to support these scores, and information from the parent interview. For example, it has been noted that he/she, even after 5 weeks in the school, is unable to find the office from the classroom without support (this is well outside the norm for language learners within our school). Also, the parents noted during interview that they do not leave him/her alone at any time, given he/she has hurt themselves accidently due to not understanding certain dangers (e.g., tried to boil water for tea and did not understand not to touch the burner to test whether or not it is hot).

2) For adverse impact, documentation of how language learning and intellectual functioning are each separately related to the adverse impact.

   Example: In addition to what is noted above, the team focused on similar problems within the student's native language. For example, he/she demonstrated a much more difficult time than his/her siblings learning the tasks within the home. The parents reported spending dramatically more time teaching him/her how to bathe, how to wash themselves, and how to brush their own teeth. Many of these tasks are still reported to be difficult, by the family. Therefore, although language learning is a portion of the adverse impact, the team, with the family, has concluded that the intellectual functioning is the primary factor. In other words, even if language learning was not an issue he/she would demonstrate significant delays in the areas of concern.

3) Does the team have evidence that the tests that were chosen to have historically worked with the noted language group?

4) Important: All of the currently available tests have issues in these areas. Non-verbal tests are normally the go-to tests. Therefore, the team can discuss choosing non-verbal IQ tests and why it is important. It is critical to understand the norming limitations of non-verbal intelligence tests, and many people, regardless of their title, do not understand the restrictions. The team can focus on using native language testing when applicable, and note its limitations. The team can also use interpreters when appropriate. In the end, the solution is never a certain test, but instead using tests that are more appropriate than others and being able to demonstrate convergent data. Does the team have evidence that the tests that were chosen to have historically worked with the noted cultural group? For

example, adaptive behavior evaluation has many weaknesses when used with students from other countries and/or cultures, given some of the items are measuring skills not expected or practiced in their country or culture.

Important: Please see the response to number 3. It is critical to think about whether or not the student had similar or different experiences than those of the normative group. Does the culture of the family value different aspects of development as more or less important than those of the normative group? Adaptive behavior can be heavily impacted by this, and the team needs be careful in supporting or negating historical and observational data on the student.

Emotional Behavioral Disability

1) Documentation of impact of language on all testing (did the student fully understand the directions).

   Example: The evaluation team has included the information from the parent interview, observation, and past records to help understand the impact of language learning on the areas tested. In the area of academic assessment, the student and family report that frustration in learning and functioning in English impact his/her willingness to try new tasks. Therefore, the results of the academic testing are impacted negatively by language learning. However, his/her parents reported that while in school in their homeland he/she demonstrated poor behaviors that led to being suspended and expelled from school.

2) For adverse impact, documentation of how language learning and the impacts of behavior are each separately related to the adverse impact.

   Example: In comparison to three other students who have similar exposure to English and who also speak Russian, his/her performance academically is the lowest within the group. Each of the other students is demonstrating delayed functioning of approximately 2 years, when tested in English, yet his/her performance is almost 4 years delayed and is at the pre-primer level. There are no other ELL students demonstrating this level of delayed academic growth, when taking into account exposure and experience.

3) Does the team have evidence of trauma?

   Example: The team, during parent interview, asked about the living conditions and experiences the family faced while in the refugee camp. The family reported that once they were in the refugee camp they felt safe and had access to adequate levels of food. They went on to report that the journey to the refugee camp was necessary due to extreme violence in their village. The team is working with the family to achieve a referral to Children's Hospital for the possible impacts of trauma.

4) If number 3 was answered yes, can the team describe (so that a stranger would understand the reasoning) how the noted impacts on learning are or are not related to the impacts of trauma?

Example: The team, in working with the parents, has chosen to implement more general education intervention while the referral and evaluation process occurs to address the potential impacts of trauma.

Other Health Impairment

1) Documentation of impact of language on all testing (did the student fully understand the directions).

Example: The team discussed with the parent his/her academic performance prior to coming to the United States. The parents noted that his/her academic performance was much lower than that of his/her peers. They report that the doctors told them that he/she had a medical condition that would make it harder for him/her to do well in school. This information supports the conclusions made by Dr. _____.

2) For adverse impact, documentation of how language learning and the impacts of the diagnosed medical condition are each separately related to the adverse impact.

Example: If he/she was not a language learner, the impact of _____ would normally be delayed skills in reading, math and written language. His/her parents have reported, and it is consistent with our school records, that the older sibling had similar schooling experiences and did not have delayed learning. Therefore, although language learning is a factor in his/her skills deficits, it is the opinion of the team that the medical condition of _____ is the primary factor in the delayed skills acquisition.

Speech or Language Impairment (SLI, sometimes referred to as a Communication Disorder or CD-Only)

1) Documentation of impact of language on all testing (did the student fully understand the directions).

Example: The team has documented through parent interview and a review of available documentation that he/she is demonstrating expressive and receptive language issues in his/her native language, that these issues have existed for a long period of time, and that these issues are not present in his/her siblings. During the testing, it was clear that the understanding of language was impacting his/her ability to understand the tasks. However, the interpreter indicated that his/her ability to understand the tasks was significantly impaired in his/her native language. Therefore, although the team cannot rule out the impact of language on understanding the evaluation tasks, it is clear that English language acquisition is an additional factor and not the primary factor.

2) Has the team documented the impact of sequential or simultaneous bilingual impact on the presenting problems?

Important: It is likely that the vast majority of students you will be evaluating will be sequential bilinguals. Therefore, this example is in regard to sequential bilinguals. Be cautious of the new definitions of simultaneous bilingual that try to argue that a student who starts a second language at 3-5 years of age is a simultaneous bilingual instead of a sequential bilingual (as though they had no language prior to that age).

Example: He/she is a sequential bilingual language learner. That is, he/she was first learning Spanish until the age of 4 with virtually no exposure to English until his/her older sibling began kindergarten. The initial exposure to English was from his/her older sibling whose English is at a beginner stage of development and is spoken with many errors. Over the course of the past year, he/she has switched from responding in Spanish to responding in English. Although the test scores represent significant delays, those delays are not uncommon at this stage of development for a sequential bilingual. Furthermore, upon using an additive language test (Bilingual Verbal Ability Test – BVAT) it was demonstrated that his/her development of language is within the norm.

3) For adverse impact, documentation of how language learning and the impacts of the noted communication disorder are each separately related to the adverse impact.

Example: He/she, as noted from the parent interview, is demonstrating significant delays within their native language with regards to expressive and receptive language. Although he/she is a sequential bilingual student, his/her delays are presenting as much more severe than those of other students with similar language experiences. Also, his/her performance on the BVAT demonstrated that using an additive approach to assessing language development still yielded data that is indicative of a delay. Therefore, although language learning cannot be ruled out as an impacting factor the team has determined that the data supports the disability as the primary factor and language acquisition as a factor that makes the adverse impact more substantial.

For both SLI and DD potential qualifications (which follows), we need to think about whether or not our current tests actually work with the groups we are using them with. That is, some of our language learners come from homes in which there is not literacy amongst the adults, some of our students come from homes in which there is poverty, and some of our students come from homes in which both are present. A lack of literacy in the home and/or poverty in the home can all have significant impacts upon the vocabulary exposure of the children. Therefore, how do we factor this in when looking at the results we are obtaining with the students we are testing? Are our results valid in these cases? Are the kids actually showing that they are doing great, given their vocabulary exposure and we just don't know?

Developmentally Delayed

1) Documentation of impact of language on all testing (did the student fully understand the directions).

   Important: Many of the examples above apply in a similar fashion to this case, the key issue and difference here is addressing the exposure, expectations, experiences, and practice as noted in number 3 below. Also, it is critical with DD and SLI to have used the Preschool Version of the ELL Critical Data Process for our preschool age students.

2) For adverse impact, documentation of how language learning and the impacts of Developmental Delays are each separately related to the adverse impact.

   Important: Many of the examples above apply to this item in a similar fashion. The difference for DD is that the team needs to focus on daily living activities in place of access to core instruction, if the student is of preschool age.

3) The team has explained (so that a stranger would understand) the impact of exposure, experience, expectations and practice on all areas of noted concern.

   Important: Even if the student is not of preschool age, the team can benefit from looking at the items on the Preschool Version of the ELL Critical Data Process. It is critical to understand how exposure, experience, expectations and practice each play into the skills a student is or is not demonstrating at this age, in addition to the impacts of being a language learner. The following is just one example write-up of one concern area.

   Example: He/she is a Spanish speaking student and within our district 84% of our ELL students are Spanish speakers. Within his/her school, there is a large ELL student population, approximately 63% of the students in the school. The neighborhoods surrounding our school have many restaurants and other businesses that can function fully in Spanish. His/her parents do not speak English. Within the school, it has been observed that he/she does not appear to be paying attention to the teacher during instruction and usually will, after instruction, ask a peer, in Spanish, what they are supposed to be doing. Therefore, he/she has very little need for English at this time and can get the majority of his/her needs met by waiting for someone to communicate with in Spanish. The team believes this lack of need has led to a significant lack of exposure, experience, and practice. Therefore, further interventions are needed at this time outside special education qualification and services.

Specific Learning Disability

1) Documentation of impact of language on all testing (did the student fully understand the directions).

   Important: The many examples above provide a number of possibilities that may apply to answer this question. It is very important that the teams use these examples to think about their specific situation, one child at a time.

2) For adverse impact, documentation of how language learning and the impacts of a SLD are each separately related to the adverse impact.

   Important: For this, too, many of the examples above provide a number of possibilities that may apply to answering this question. It is very important that the teams use these examples to think about their specific situation, one child at a time.

3) Documentation of learning disability: like information from previous educational setting in student's native language.

   Important: This is a critical factor for all students who are in the early development stages of English language acquisition. Without this, the team needs to collect massive additional supporting data from other sources. Other sources of data that should always be present, but need to be stronger for the student who does not have documented learning problems in a previous educational setting are: language acquisition rates as compared to peers (significantly slower), targeted intervention data rates of growth as compared to peers (significantly slower), other learning tasks data rates of growth as compared to peers (significantly slower), and parent interview data that is supportive of learning problems. If the data regarding the previous setting is available, it might be written up as follows:

   Example: In his/her previous educational setting in his/her homeland there are documented concerns regarding the rate of learning to read, write and do math. The parents report frequent conversations with his/her teachers regarding the lack of progress in reading, math and writing. The parents report that their child attended school just like the older siblings, who did not struggle to learn these skills. The parents had one report card, and the report card documents very low performance in these areas and the teacher's comment was that he/she was attending regularly, well behaved, and putting forth a consistent effort in class.

4) Documentation of slower rates of language acquisition as compared to like peers.

   Example: The state testing scores for language acquisition for _____ were compared to the scores of three other students in the same grade who have been learning English for the same length of time and speak the same language as _____. The language acquisition rates for the other three students all demonstrate a strong upward growth curve for English language learning, yet his/her growth in English language learning is well below that of the comparison students. Also, compared to other students who have been evaluated in the past, he/she is demonstrating English language acquisition rates similar to the students who were eventually qualified for special education services. It is important to note that _____ Elementary has evaluated its data regarding qualification rates of ELL students and has one of the lower qualification rates within the district and has no areas of disproportionality. Therefore, the comparison to previously evaluated and qualified students is deemed to be an appropriate comparison.

5) Documentation of slower rates of learning on other tasks as compared to like peers.

   Example: He/she was compared to three other ELL students in Mr. Smith's PE classroom, with regards to the rate in which they learned the rules of a new game. Mr. Smith was not provided the name of the student of concern, in an effort to minimize possible impact on the scores. Mr. Smith was simply asked to rate each of the students on a 1-5 scale regarding his perception of how quickly they learned the rules of the new games, each time a new game was presented. The scores for the 4 students indicate that he/she is learning the rules of the new games at the same rate as the other students. Therefore, this data is not supportive of a suspected learning disability.

Examples for Reports (based on ELL Critical Data Process item number)

The following paragraphs provide language you may use to help you write content in Special Education Evaluation Reports **as related to the ELL Critical Data Process**

Item #4 --- Expected Years of Education

In order to rule-out lack of appropriate instruction in reading or math, the team needs to consider the student's education history in these areas. If a student has received formal education/schooling in their native language, that will go a long way toward answering these questions. The team then needs to know whether or not the student was successful, how consistently they attended school, and how they performed in comparison to their peers and relatives. If the evidence clearly shows that they attended school the expected amount of time, that most students were successful, and that their relatives were successful, yet the student struggled to learn, then the team has clear evidence to support the possibility of a Specific Learning Disability.

The possibility of a Specific Learning Disability is very hard to determine if the evidence clearly shows no education/schooling in the student's native language, unless many of the issues listed below, that are indicative of a disability, are present. All of the possibilities between these two ends of the spectrum have related levels of need for other evidence (i.e., more evidence is needed the closer you are to no schooling and less evidence is needed the closer you are to appropriate schooling with little success compared to peers and relatives).

The question arises regarding children born in the United States with no schooling/education in their native language. Many of these children are the children most impacted by language and least likely to be impacted by disability. As noted before, these students must overcome (in many cases) the lack of need for English outside the school setting, sometimes even within the school setting, and the impacts of not having the formal education/schooling in their native language, so that they can transfer that learning to their new learning. Additionally, many language learners have to overcome having learned English incorrectly. And, correcting the mistakes of learning any skill incorrectly takes a great deal of effort (all while also trying to learn content in English).

The lack of transferable skills is a major challenge that creates a competition for learning time. For example, the teacher might be teaching a lesson on the usage of certain verbs to create different emphasis and there are language learners in the room who have been taught this material before as well as language learners who do not know the concepts of verbs and nouns as used in school terms. Therefore, one student is transferring prior learning to the new language (as soon as they know that verb means _____ in their language) and the other student is wondering what a verb is and trying to create a meaning for whenever the teacher uses the word, usually then missing out on the actual lesson.

Item #4 Examples

1) Student did receive education in native language in country of origin.

Jose attended school in Mexico during his kindergarten through second grade school years and has attended school here in Seattle during his third and fourth grade school years. Jose's parents indicated that Jose attended school regularly, only missing school if he was ill. Jose's parents and the limited records available indicate that Jose's performance was below average, using his grades of _____ and his parents' comments that he did not do as well in school as his siblings as evidence.

This would be supportive of eligibility.

2) Student did not receive education in native language.

Maria was born in the United States and received no schooling in Spanish. Maria is now a second-grade student in Renton and she has not received any formal education in Spanish. Maria entered school as a Spanish speaker with very limited prior exposure to English.

This is an example that would not be supportive of eligibility for special education services. The primary issue is that Maria does not have the skills students learn during formal schooling to transfer to her learning English and the lack of formal support in Spanish has been shown (see Collier and Thomas) to have poor educational outcomes.

Item #6 --- Student did not learn to read in their primary language

The team needs to know whether or not the student had a real opportunity to learn to read in their primary language. If a student had a real opportunity to learn to read in their primary language and did learn to read in their primary language, it is unlikely that they will get referred for a special education evaluation. The students who did not learn to read in their primary language need to be examined across a spectrum of possibilities.

The spectrum runs from the student who had a strong educational history in which most children (their peers and relatives) learned to read, yet they did not learn to read, to children who had little opportunity to learn to read (and most of their peers and relatives did not learn to read). A student who fits the category of having the opportunities and their peers/relatives learned to read; however, the student did not, is a student whose evidence points toward a Specific Learning Disability. A student who fits the category of having minimal opportunity and their peers/relatives did not learn to read does not have evidence supportive of qualification as a student with a Specific Learning Disability.

Item #6 Examples

1) Student did not learn to read in native language and was not reasonably exposed to reading in native language.

Boris sporadically attended school during his kindergarten through the 3rd grade school years. His parents needed to move multiple times during this timeframe, and sometimes did not enroll him into school prior to making the next move. Boris, according to his parents, did not learn to read in Russian. Boris' parents noted that they were unable to help him learn to read during this time, that he had very little instruction in reading, and that none of his siblings with similar experiences learned to read in Russian.

This is an example that does not support qualification.

2) Student did not learn to read in native language and was given significant exposure and instruction to reading in native language.

Natanya consistently attended school in Russia from Kindergarten through the third grade. Natanya's parents are concerned that she did not learn the basic skills in reading that were expected of other students her age, the skills her older siblings had mastered in the same system by the same age. Natanya's parents and siblings read to her and with her, but indicated that Natanya struggles to grasp the concepts of reading and that she reads very slowly, mispronouncing many of the words.

This is an example that would be supportive of qualification.

No example was provided for a student who did learn to read in native language for two reasons. First, we rarely see them when SLD is a consideration. Second, learning to read in Primary or Native Language is a strong predictor of success in a following language.

Item #7 --- Years Learning English

This item is related to the work by Dr. Jim Cummins, Dr. Collier and Dr. Thomas. There is a great deal of evidence that documents that students need 5-7 years to be relatively competitive in our educational system. This relies heavily upon the quality of the ELL services delivered (please review the work of Dr. Collier and Dr. Thomas on this topic). A student with less than this amount of time would need a great deal of evidence from targeted interventions (that have historically worked for other language learners) to support a qualification under the category of Specific Learning Disability.

Item #7 Examples

1) Student does not have the 5-7 years of learning English, yet qualification is a reasonable potential option.

Ahmed has been in the United States and learning English for 3 years. Ahmed's progress on language acquisition testing is far below that of his peers who speak the same language and who have been in the United States receiving education for the same period of time. Targeted reading intervention has been given to Ahmed and 3 of his peers with similar issues in learning to read, and who have been learning English for the same period of time. Ahmed's peer group during the interventions has made significantly more progress, yet Ahmed has demonstrated very little progress during repeated intervention cycles. Furthermore, Ahmed's PE teacher has been systematically monitoring his learning of new games in comparison to other language learners and Ahmed is demonstrating far more difficulty.

2) Student does not have the 5-7 years, and qualification is not a likely option.

Amira has been in the United States and learning English for 4 years. Her progress on language acquisition testing is similar to that of her peers who speak the same language and who have been in the United States receiving formal education for approximately the same period of time. Amira has been receiving targeted reading intervention and her rate of growth, when compared to her peers (same language, similar time learning English), is roughly equivalent.

Item #8 --- Attendance History

It is very difficult to make progress and do well in school with poor attendance. Early warning systems for academic failure are now becoming common across the country. Find out whether or not your district has this in place, and, if so, what they consider the warning levels for excused and unexcused absences. There is research that indicates 3 unexcused or 15 excused/unexcused combined is indicative of long term problems. The team needs to know the "why" for the absences in order to respond to this item. Is the student absent because school is now hard for them and they do not see a way to be successful or are they absent because school has always been hard for them?

Item #8 Examples

1) Student whose data is supportive of eligibility

Lin has missed a great deal of school this year.* Our school has a 98% attendance rate and only 0.5% of the students have either 3 unexcused absences or more than 9 total absences. When Lin was interviewed, it was made clear that the high absenteeism is due to not believing that school is a place where success can be found. Lin's parents noted that Lin has struggled far more in school than the other children, and that absenteeism has always been a problem.

* Give the actual number of days when you write it.

2) Student whose data is not supportive of eligibility

May has missed a great deal of school this year.* Our school has a 98% attendance rate and only 0.5% of the students have either 3 unexcused absences or more than 9 total absences. When May was interviewed, it was clear that she was missing school due to a lack of understanding that attendance is required. May and the principal discussed this at length, and May was unaware of this as an expectation.

* Give the actual number of days when you write it.

Focus on whether or not the absenteeism is related to school being hard for the student in general, as opposed to learning English and performing in English being hard for the student. This is where parent and student interviews, with a strong emphasis on historical performance and sibling comparisons, is very important.

Item #9 --- Approach Taken with Regards to ELL Services

The only approaches that show positive results at systems levels involve native language support. Anything less relies on teachers who can beat the odds, and what happens when they move on to a new opportunity?

Item #9 Examples:

1) Student whose data is supportive of eligibility

Johnny is attending a school in which a dual language program has been developed over a 10 year period of time. During this time, the school has seen the qualification rates of language learners drop to levels equal to the rates of non-language learners and the language acquisition scores are the highest within the school district. Johnny, though, is not acquiring English language skills at the rate of his peers and is, in fact, struggling greatly on tasks that the average students in this setting master within roughly ½ the amount of time it takes him.

2) Student whose data is supportive of eligibility

Joe is attending a school that, although not using research proven methods of ELL service delivery, has a long history of success with ELL students. That is, the students in Mrs. Jones' classroom are consistently outperforming all other students within the school district on state language acquisition tests, and local reading and math testing. Joe's rates of language acquisition, and reading and math scores, are within the lowest 5% of the scores for language learners in our school over the past 10 years.

3) Student whose data is not supportive of eligibility (important- this example is common. However, how long someone has done something is not a critical factor, their results are critical. Also, opinions of experts can be valuable if the teacher has proven results. Data trumps opinion).

Julie is attending _____ Elementary. Our teacher has been teaching language learners for 27 years and has stated that Julie is one of the slowest progressing language learners that she has experienced.

Item #10 --- Rate of Growth on the State Language Acquisition Testing

When compared to peers with a similar background (language, exposure, experience...) how does this student's growth curve look on this testing? If it is similar to that of other students, this is evidence against the likelihood of qualification for a Specific Learning Disability. If the rate of growth is far lower than that of peers, then this is evidence that supports the qualification of the student under the category of a Specific Learning Disability.

Item #10 Examples:

1) Student whose data is supportive of eligibility

Alberto's language acquisition rate was compared to that of three other students who speak the same native language and who have been learning English for approximately the same period of time. This was determined by charting the language acquisition scores for each of the students over a three year period of time. The rate of growth for Alberto is the slowest of the four students, and the other three students all have similar growth curves that represent much faster language acquisition.

2) Student whose data is not supportive of eligibility.

Alicia's language acquisition rate was compared to that of three other students who speak the same native language and who have been learning English for approximately the same period of time. This was determined by charting the language acquisition scores for each of the students over a three year period of time. The rate of growth for Alicia is similar to that of the other three students, and the growth curve of the scores for Alicia represents the second fastest rate of acquisition within this group of students.

Item #11 --- Targeted Intervention History

This is a critical item, especially when the student does not reach the 5-7 year threshold noted above. The team needs to examine how the student of concern responded to an intervention that was targeted to the specific need, and was provided for a minimum of 10 weeks with intensity and fidelity. It is important to be able to document how the team knows for sure that the intervention actually targeted the specific need of the student of concern (no guessing, actual facts). Then, look at the growth curves. A growth curve similar to that of the other students with similar needs (and similar language learning backgrounds) indicates that qualification under the category of Specific Learning Disability is likely not the appropriate decision. A growth curve significantly below that of other students with similar needs and language backgrounds is indicative of potential qualification under the category of Specific Learning Disability.

Item #11 Examples:

1) Student whose data is supportive of eligibility

Alexio was provided a targeted intervention in the area of reading, more specifically phonemic awareness skills. This area was chosen based upon Alexio demonstrating the lowest skills in this area for a second-grade student, during the universal screening completed by the school. Alexio was grouped with three other students who demonstrated the same concern and who are all language learners. Two of these students speak the same native language as Alexio: one has been learning English slightly longer and one has been learning English for a slightly shorter period of time. One student does not speak the same language as Alexio, but speaks a language that has roughly the same number of native speakers and has been learning English for the same length of time as Alexio. Alexio's skills in this area were measured before the intervention, as well as 4 times during the intervention, and 3 days after the intervention was completed. Alexio's rate of growth on this intervention was the slowest rate of growth of the 4 students and was significantly below the rate of growth of the other three students (who all demonstrated similar rates of growth).

2) Student whose data is not supportive of eligibility

Alexandria was provided a targeted intervention in the area of reading, more specifically phonemic awareness skills. This area was chosen based upon Alexandria demonstrating the lowest skills in this area for a second-grade student, during the universal screening completed by the school. Alexandria was grouped with three other students who demonstrated the same concern and who are all language learners. Two of these students speak the same native language as Alexandra: one has been learning English slightly longer and one has been learning English for a slightly shorter period of time. Alexandria's skills in this area were measured before the intervention, 4 times during the intervention, and 3 days after the intervention was completed. Alexandria's rate of growth on this intervention was similar to that of the other 3 students. In fact, she had the strongest growth curve of the four students.

Item #12 --- Expectations in the General Education Classroom

If the student has not been required to turn in homework at all times in which other students have had the requirement, then the team has evidence supporting qualification under the category of Specific Learning Disability. If the student has had the requirement and made an effort at all times, yet there has been little progress or growth, then the team has evidence that the student would not qualify under the category of Specific Learning Disability.

Item #12 Examples:

1) Student whose data is supportive of eligibility

Jimmy is a student in Mrs. Johnson's classroom. Mrs. Johnson's classroom is a well-run classroom. Students in her classroom are on task, as measured during observations, 94% of the time. Also, the test scores for Mrs. Johnson on state testing are consistently above those of 3rd grade students across the school district. In Mrs. Johnson's classroom, Jimmy is expected to complete assignments at all times in which other students are expected to complete assignments. Mrs. Johnson, knowing Jimmy struggles in school, began the school year allowing Jimmy to complete the assignments at a lower level than other students, while supporting Jimmy and raising the expectations consistently. Jimmy has made some growth over time with respect to completing assignments that are closer to the rubrics Mrs. Johnson has for the students in her classroom. However, Jimmy's work is still at the lowest level of the students in Mrs. Johnson's classroom.

2) Student whose data is not supportive of eligibility

Cindy is a student in Mr. Jones' classroom. During observation, the students in Mr. Jones' classroom are on-task approximately 65% of the time. Also, the observer who did not know Cindy, was unable to pick Cindy out from the other students when completing a "blind" observation. Upon completing a second observation, and knowing who Cindy was from the beginning of the observation, the data indicated that Cindy is on-task at the same percentage as other students in the classroom. When Mr. Jones was interviewed, he stated that Cindy does not turn in many of her assignments, he guessed that it was over 50%. Mr. Jones was unsure, given that he sometimes gives Cindy a passing grade on an assignment when she participates in the classroom without disrupting. This indicates that the integrity of the grades limits the ability to use the grades as evidence.

Item #14 --- Comparison Student Data

This is the other data, like science test scores or team created data, that the team found as a way to monitor and measure the student's rate of learning (this is not about reading, math or written language, given those are addressed in the targeted interventions). This might be a PE or music teacher keeping data on their perceived rate of learning a new game. This might be the classroom teacher keeping data on something that is measurable, but not reading, math, written language, or language acquisition, given each of these is documented above. Then, the team will make its decision based on how the student is learning the new skill or knowledge as compared to language learning peers.

Item #14 Examples:

1) Student whose data is supportive of eligibility

Brad's PE teacher, Mr. Ellis, worked with the school psychologist to create a systematic way to monitor and score his students on how quickly they are learning the rules of each new game. Mr. Ellis kept data on Brad and three other language learners who had a similar amount of time learning English. Brad's scores over the course of learning three new games were the lowest of the comparison group overall, and Brad was not scored higher than any other student during any of the new games.

Important: Remember, this works the best if the PE/music teacher does not know which student is the student of concern.

2) Student whose data is not supportive of eligibility

Suzie's PE teacher, Mr. Ellis, worked with the school psychologist to create a systematic way to monitor and score his students on how quickly they are learning the rules of each new game. Mr. Ellis kept data on Suzie and three other language learners who had a similar amount of time learning English. Suzie's scores regarding how quickly she learned the rules of the new games were within the average of the students measured. Also, Suzie was the fastest to learn the rules of 4 Square.

Items #15 and #16 --- Parent Interview Items

One goal for the interviews is to learn whether or not something critical has not otherwise been considered. Is there a medical condition that was not noted that needs to be considered (then the discussion could need to turn toward Other Health Impairment)? Is there a family history of learning difficulties? Please note, a parent or sibling with a disability is not a 1-to-1 relationship to this child having a disability. If the sibling or parent is accurately identified (which we know is highly problematic with language learners), then there is a correlational relationship (the strength of which varies based upon the disability).

Items #15 and #16 Examples:

1) Student whose data is supportive of eligibility

Xavier's parents stated during the parent interview that many of the family members have found school to be very difficult. They noted that although their friends were learning to read well in school, they had had many difficulties learning to read. Also, Xavier demonstrated a more difficult time learning his age appropriate self-help skills as compared to his cousins.

75

2) Student whose data is supportive of eligibility

David's parents stated that they had had many doctors' appointments in their home country when David was a child. They stated that the doctors had told them that David would have a more difficult time learning and that school would be difficult for him, due to the medical problems. The family was unsure of the diagnosis, but stated they had paperwork in their native language that might have the information. The school psychologist made a copy of the paperwork, and worked with a trained interpreter/translator to both talk with the family and translate the documents. The translator was asked to look for any medical diagnosis and any statements regarding the possible impacts of the medical conditions. The translator provided the school psychologist a list of medical diagnoses documented in the paperwork and the statements by the doctors regarding the possible impact on learning.

3) Student whose data is not supportive of eligibility

Stephanie's parents reported that she met developmental milestones at the same rate as her siblings and cousins. They noted that there is no history of learning problems within any of the family members and that Stephanie has had no injuries or illness of any significance.

Chapter 7: Using the ELL Critical Data Process for Interventions, Referrals, or Special Education Evaluations

This chapter is designed to provide a few examples of how the data could be used to design interventions, support a referral for special education services or support a special education evaluation. The discussions that occur during the ELL Critical Data Process are not meant to simply figure out where to put the check mark, the discussions should lead the team to ideas for areas in which to create interventions or to data needed to support the processing of a special education referral. And if the team proposes a special education evaluation (and obtains the parent's consent), some of this data is needed to increase the likelihood of an accurate evaluation of a language learner.

For each of the items, the authors randomly chose to address certain areas. The authors have seen where too much information leads teams into trying to fit their situation into a box, instead of using the examples to help guide them. Therefore, in this section, we only provide some examples to provoke thought.

For many of the items, the discussion under Referral and Evaluation will be very similar. That is, in most cases you and your team are trying to decide if the weight of the evidence across many points supports a referral, and possibly at a later date whether the weight of the items, when combined with assessment data, supports a disability. If the student has a clear disability that is rarely impacted by language learning (i.e., the determinant factor is the disability and not the lack of English language acquisition), then these discussions are rather easy. This is the case for disabilities like blindness, deafness, and severe intellectual disabilities (what appears to be a mild intellectual disability could be something else, though). The majority of the problems, when teams will struggle most, are in the "soft" categories like specific learning disability, speech or language impairment, and developmental delay. Therefore, if any of these categories is the possible outcome of an evaluation, the data needs to be stronger and more clear-cut, given the disability is not.

The like peer group provides stronger data the more the peers are like the student of concern regarding language spoken, time in the US, type of ELL services provided, etcetera. However, there will be times in which finding like peers is very difficult. For "rare" students, meaning there are no other students who speak the same language within the setting, these students tend to be less commonly referred and/or qualified (there is less disproportionality data within these groups), the team just needs to find other students who are less common linguistically, but match for other factors like time learning English. Do not use students from commonly found linguistic groups within your district as comparison students for the less commonly found linguistic groups. Then, if you are in a very small district, work with your agency (e.g., ESD or AEA) to find like peers.

K-12 Version

Item number 1: Student's Primary Language Characteristics

Intervention: If the student is a Spanish speaking student, and lives in a community in which they can easily speak Spanish the vast majority of the time, it is likely that they need interventions that are designed to increase their vocabulary. Also, since they might not have any formal education in Spanish and may not be reading in Spanish, they may need vocabulary development in both English and Spanish.

If the student speaks a language other than English, and you have a specific example of them struggling with a skill that many students who speak that language and are learning English struggle with, the team needs to create an intervention that targets the specific concern. For example, many students who speak Asian languages, there is over qualification for speech and language services in the area of articulation. In place of special education qualification, the SLP could use the 5 Minute Artic method and do this as an RTI service outside of special education qualification.

Item number 2: Student who speaks multiple languages

Intervention: During the process of interviewing the family (and possibly the student), it is possible that the team will find information that indicates something the student is struggling with that has a negative impact on their ability to focus on learning. This could be a cultural issue or trauma. If the student is a student who has suffered trauma, the team can find resources in the area for trauma treatment and provide the contact information to the family. If there is a cultural issue, the team can find a leader in the community of the family and ask for ideas and/or help to assist the student. As a reminder, a student who speaks multiple languages and is not learning English probably has a root problem that is not related to their ability to learn new languages. Therefore, the team is looking for that root problem.

Item number 3: Language Confusion

For this example, language confusion is defined as: The student is unsure of which words go with which language. For example, a student knows "red" is the correct word when they see something red, but does not know which language "red" goes with. This same student might know that something is "azul" when they see something blue, but they don't know which language "azul" goes with. This student might be able to pick out some of the colors if you ask the questions in Spanish, and other colors when you ask in English. The student might answer at times in English at times in Spanish. This is contrasted to randomly inserting English words into their Spanish or Spanish words into their English, which could be a lack of vocabulary in one language or the other, and for some students with stronger language skills this could be code switching.

Evaluation: During a special education evaluation, the team takes their pre-referral data and combines the data with evaluation data. A student who is struggling with language confusion at 8 years of age is a supporting piece of data, yet not extremely strong. However, a 14-year-old student who has been exposed since birth to the two languages in question, and the exposure has been strong for both languages, whose siblings have none of the same problems, is a student for whom this piece of data is strong and supportive of a potential disability.

Item number 4 - Red Flag Area!: Education in Native/Primary language

Intervention: If the student has not had the exposure and experiences to formal education in their native language they are missing the transferable skills from their language to the English language. They are also missing the school exposure in a language in which they always knew what was occurring. Therefore, if at all possible, we need to provide them support and learning opportunities in their native language. If there are things they can do in their native language, we need to find ways to make this work for them (e.g., iPad or iPhone with iTranslate). Also, if we see them struggling with something that is a normal school activity, we need to assume they don't know what is expected instead of thinking they "can't" do it correctly. With this, we need to teach the skill and observe how quickly they learn the new skill in a way they can understand. Part of the intervention can be the effective use of technology and translanguaging.

Item number 5: Parental literacy in primary language

Intervention: Students whose parents are not literate in the language they use with their children need activities designed to build vocabulary. And, in most cases, would benefit from vocabulary building in both languages. If at all possible, use picture dictionaries that have both languages, then the vocabulary is more comprehensible and the parents can help with the vocabulary building (since they know the names of the items, even if they cannot read them in their primary language).

Referral: If this was marked at or toward referral, it is because the student has literate parents, who read to them, and the student is struggling to learn academically. This is one point of data that helps the team understand that the student is having a struggle that does not appear reasonable given their exposure/experience/expectations/practice. Now, the team needs to compare and contrast this against the other points of data to see if the totality of information supports asking the parents to consent for a special education evaluation or not.

Item number 6 - Red Flag Area!: Student did not learn to read in the primary language

Intervention: More intervention is marked in this case because the student didn't have a reasonable opportunity to learn to read in their native language, and they are trying to learn to read in English while they are trying to learn English. Any type of native language support at this time would be very helpful in linking transferable knowledge. For example, being able to listen to the same story in their native language prior to needing to listen to or read it in English is going to increase comprehension. If they have the option to use an electronic device that can translate portions of text into their native language and provide an audio clip in their native language, that would be helpful. Some students just need help with a handful of words per page. So, if they have a device they can use to quickly find the meaning of a word in their native language (especially if they can hear the word) they will have more success. For the last two suggestions, iPhones and iPads have iTranslate available that can be used with voice (something very helpful with newcomers for the teachers and front office staff).

Item number 7 - Red Flag Area!: Years learning English

Please note, we don't delay referrals to special education, even one day, for students who are language learners and have a disability that clearly has no relationship to language acquisition and almost always leads to special education services for native English speakers, like students who have blindness or deafness.

Evaluation: During a special education evaluation, the team takes their pre-referral data and combines it with evaluation data. If you have a student who has been in the school in the United States for 6-7 years and is doing poorly in school, you potentially have a student with a disability. To use this to support a potential disability, you need to know more about the students in your school system who speak the same language as this student. If there is a group of LTELs (Long Term ELLs) who are not making progress in your system and not graduating at the same rate, then this is not strong evidence toward supporting a disability (if the student of concern is part of this group). In contrast, this data supports eligibility for students from very low incidence languages who are struggling, given their need to learn English is much greater (investigate to make sure this is true for the student of concern).

Item number 8: Attendance History

Intervention: If the student is not attending school, and you are able to determine that they are not attending due to school being a bad experience for them or because of a belief that school is not mandatory, then the team can work with the student to address their concerns. For example, if a student is not attending school because they have always done well in school and suddenly they are struggling, they need to be able to talk with others who have had the same experience and succeeded. These students need to know that studying in a new language and a new culture is a difficult task for everyone. If you have a student who is not attending due to a cultural belief that school is not important or is optional, then help them to see the options that can open up for them if they continue with school. Do not disparage their thinking, but instead provide them information on what is possible if they stay in school.

Referral: If you have a student who is struggling in school and school has always been difficult for this student, then the team needs to look for evidence that supports this claim. The stronger the evidence the more likely that a decision will be easier and clearer during the referral process. This is one point of data that helps the team understand that the student's struggle does not appear reasonable given their exposure/experience/expectations/practice. Now, the team needs to compare and contrast this against the other points of data to see if the totality of information supports asking the parents to consent for a special education evaluation or not.

Item number 9: Approach taken with regards to ELL services

It is not uncommon for students to struggle in a dual language program until early to late third grade (e.g., language confusion) and then to perform at a much higher level (a delay versus a disability).

Referral: If you have a strong ELL system, based upon data, and you have a student who is doing poorly, then how strong is your data and how much does this support a potential disability and the need to complete a special education evaluation? The more the student is "sticking out" from other students, the more this supports moving forward, the less they "stick out", the more you would need strong indicators in other items to support moving forward. This is one point of data that helps the team understand whether or not the student's struggle appears reasonable given their exposure/experience/expectations/practice. Now, the team needs to compare and contrast this against the other points of data to see if the totality of information supports asking the parents to consent for a special education evaluation or not.

Evaluation: During a special education evaluation, the team takes their pre-referral data and combines it with evaluation data. The more the student is "sticking out" from other students, the more this supports moving forward, the less they "stick out," the more you would need strong indicators in other items to support the possibility of special education eligibility.

Item number 10 - Red Flag Area!: Rate of growth on the state language acquisition test

Evaluation: This is a key piece of data if you are evaluating a language learner who you believe might have a specific learning disability, and has less than the 5-7 years learning English. This can be combined with other points of data as an indicator of how well this student learns in comparison to like peers. The farther below the rate of learning of their like peers, the stronger the data becomes. In contrast, the closer their rate of learning to their like peers, the weaker the data becomes relative to a potential disability.

Item number 11 - Red Flag Area!: Intervention Description

Intervention: This can be a key to either generating intervention ideas or to deciding in favor of a referral and possibly an evaluation. That is, if you complete a targeted intervention and the student performs in a manner similar to like peers your team needs to keep doing what they are doing.

In contrast....

Referral: This could be moderate to strong data for either the referral decision or during the evaluation process. If the student performed poorly on a targeted intervention when compared to like peers, and there is other supporting data to go from referral to proposing an evaluation for special education, then this could be a piece of data supporting that decision.

Targeted intervention is a key to understanding a student who you might believe there is a possibility of a specific learning disability, especially when the student is under that 5 years of experience learning English. However, if they are within an LTEL (Long-term ELL) group, the evaluations become much more difficult and the system needs to examine ways in which to reduce the quantity of LTEL students through more effective ELL services.

Item number 12: Expectations in the general education classroom

Intervention: The intervention in this case should be obvious, the team needs to work together to create reasonable expectations and a support system for the expectations (with reasonable modifications as the student's skills grow).

Item number 13: Classroom observation

Referral: If you have a student who is in a well-run classroom, who is trying to follow along with the other students, who is just not progressing in a manner similar to their like peers, your team needs to see whether or not there are other data points that indicate a similar trend. This is a potential piece of data that can be indicative of a student's rate of learning or ease of ability to learn. It would be important to note how other language learners are doing in the same classroom. The more unlike the other students this student is, the more supportive this data is of going from referral to proposing a special education evaluation. If there are other language learners in that setting who are struggling then this is not a strong piece of data.

Item number 14: Comparison Student Data

In the Music/PE example the Music and/or PE teacher is provided with a chart of 4-5 students, as similar as possible, that includes the student of concern, and the teacher has to rate each student on a 1-5 scale. This would occur right after class and the teacher would rate the student from 1 (struggled greatly to learn the new lesson) to 5 (learned the new lesson quickly). The teacher should not know which of the students is the student of concern.

Evaluation: This is another key piece of data in the referral and evaluation process. This is especially important for the evaluations in which the team is looking at the possibility of a qualification in the category of specific learning disability for a student who has less than the 5-7 years of learning English. Again, the more unlike this student is than their true peers, the stronger this supports qualification. The less unlike this student is than their true peers, the less this supports qualification.

Item numbers 15 and 16: The Parent Interview – Red Flag Area! – and   Developmental History:

For both of these items, the interventions are not likely to be designed from this new knowledge, but instead due to this new knowledge. In some cases (unless you find out about a medical condition previously unknown or the student clearly has a disability), you might go straight to intervention. For example, if you find out the student has never been in school before, it is likely that you need to find a way to provide some of those early school experiences while providing age appropriate experiences (in other words, more schooling). At other times, the data from these items could lead straight to evaluation. This could be finding out that the student has a medical condition that is almost always directly linked to a need for special education services.

Preschool Version

Please note, the first few items/examples are going to focus on interventions. For the later items the authors used more examples for "referral" or "evaluation." That is not because those items lead that direction to a greater degree, but instead to provide a balance of examples.

Exposure (1):

Intervention: In this case, if a child has not been exposed to a desired learning, or not exposed to the extent that other children who learned the skill have been exposed, then exposure is needed. There are times in which the lack of exposure is related to cultural issues. Therefore, the team needs to be respectful of this and think about alternative exposures that could provide the same skill development. For example, some mothers feed their children and do not encourage their children to feed themselves. This could lead to slower development of some fine-motor skills (and low scores on some of our rating scales and potentially have no relationship to a disability). Instead of debating with the parents regarding the choices they are making, the team could suggest toys that require fine-motor skills development.

Experience (2):

Intervention: In this case, if a student has not had the experience, then they need the experience. The example above crossed over from Exposure to Experience by suggesting having the student play with different types of toys. This would not only give them the exposure, but also the experience (and do so in a fun way that they are likely to stay involved with, which adds in Practice).

Expectations in the household/daycare (3):

Intervention: In this case, there are times in which the parents need to be provided with ideas (interventions) so they understand the impact of their behaviors on reinforcing their children, for both the positive and not so positive results. For example, with children who grunt to get their needs met in place of using language, the parents are meeting the needs of the child without any expectations regarding attempting language, and the child really has little or no need to develop the skills. Therefore, the team (continued below in item 4) can work with the parents regarding an intervention, and they would then create reasonable expectations for the child for the area of concern.

Intervention (Practice) Description (4):

Intervention: This example is continued from above. The team could help the parents to understand what key words to start expecting the child to produce (the highly motivating words related to the child getting their wants and needs met). The team could talk with the parents regarding reinforcing correct approximations, shaping the words with the child, and the fact that the child might have some tantrums at first (given what they were doing was working for them and they cannot understand the need for a change).

Referral: The parent from the situation noted above, regarding speech, followed through with your recommendations and the child is still struggling. This would be a potential piece of data supporting marking referral in the matrix and processing the referral. If the discussions with the parent during the referral led to information that they were inconsistent, then the team might refuse to propose an evaluation (and work with the parents regarding the intervention). If the team learned that the parents were very consistent and the child made very little growth, the team might choose to propose an evaluation.

Evaluation: In this case, if there was a targeted intervention that was completed with fidelity and the child made much slower than expected growth (when compared to like peers), this could be a strong piece of data (depending upon the other sources of data and how well it either fits in with those pieces of data or does not).

Parental literacy in primary language (5):

Referral: If you find out that the parents have strong literacy skills, that they read with and talked with their child as they did with their other children, and their other children are developing as expected, yet this child is not, then you have strong evidence to combine with your other sources of data during the referral process.

Approach taken with regards to English Learning (6):

Evaluation: If you have a child who has had significant exposure to learning English, has motivation to learn English (e.g. loves the cartoons in English and wants to speak English with older siblings), but is struggling to learn English, then you might have evidence that supports the possibility that this child has a disability. The key issue is how this combines with other sources of data. If the other sources of data conflict with this, then the team needs to determine why (is there another cause for the problem that the team does not know).

Child's Primary Language, Environment, and Need to Learn English (7):

Referral: If you have a child who has a significant need to develop English language skills and has the exposure to these skills, and is not learning the English, then you have a piece of data that could support the referral process. For example, if the child speaks a native language that is extremely uncommon in your area (and nobody other than their family speaks this language) and the child is in a daycare environment in which nobody speaks their language, and they still are not learning English, this could be strong evidence during the referral process.

Observation (8):

Intervention: Your team completes an observation and the child behaves appropriately with children they have never seen before and listens to the requests of the adults (other than their parents) and completes the requests, then you probably need to discuss an intervention with the parents. That is, if a child can get along with children in general (just not their siblings) and listens well to adults (just not their parents), then someone needs to find the nicest way possible to point this out to the family. Then, if that goes well, the staff and parents can talk about parenting skills and strategies.

The Parent Interview (9 A) and **Developmental History (9 B):**

The parent interview and developmental history have the possibility of discovering information that leads directly toward intervention or evaluation. For example, if the team learns about a medical condition that almost always leads to the need for special education services, then the team might go directly to making a special education referral. In contrast, the team might learn about a history of trauma and work to find information and resources to link the family with.

Like in the K-12 process, each time the team looks at the skill that needs to be developed, they are trying to determine how to intervene upon developing that skill or how well this piece of data supports other pieces of data in the referral and/or evaluation process. Allow the student data, not your beliefs or preconceptions, to determine which path is travelled. Only your overall school student data will tell you how much your beliefs or your preconceptions have impacted your work ("you" meaning all people involved in the process).

Chapter 8: Eligibility Categories and Challenges

The referral process has led to the decision to evaluate and the parents have provided permission. The team has completed the ELL Critical Data Process. Now you need to take that information and integrate it with more data.

First, we will narrow down our thought process by looking at the eligibility categories. Earlier in this book you will find examples of the types and qualities of data that strengthens or weakens cases. In the following pages, we will examine four groups of eligibility categories. These groups were chosen based on the examination of disproportionality by disability category, from highest to lowest.

Each section will list the disability or disabilities that fall within that section and then describe some of the problems and challenges teams will face. The order of the sections is from the most problematic category to the least problematic categories. The final section has information that is somewhat repetitive, given that there is far less disproportionality in those categories and fewer challenges faced by the teams. Teams almost always correctly identify when a student has blindness or deafness. Some folks laugh at that last sentence and some are offended, sadly, though, it really is "only" almost always and not always.

The most problematic category with the most disproportionality

- Specific Learning Disability

Below are a series of quotes that I use when providing training in this area. For each quote I am providing additional information. Each team needs to know that there is research to support that the vast majority of the children who are incorrectly identified for special education are identified within the category of Specific Learning Disability.

This is a category that was, more or less, created for the special education world. It is the only category that greatly increased beyond population change from 1975 to 2004, when the special education population in the United States peaked between 2000 and 2004, and has since been dropping. It is the main category to decrease in size since 2004. The SLD category tripled in numbers from 1975 to 2004, eventually being the category in which roughly 50% of all special education students were qualified. Interestingly enough, the decrease in this category started with the federal law that included the usage of RTI qualification. It is easy to see the decrease in the SLD category aligning with the increased usage of RTI within the school systems. At last check, SLD now represents roughly 38.8% of all students qualified for special education (This was written in 2017 looking at the most current OSEP published data).

The following quotes provide a lot to think about and are followed by ways to mitigate the majority of these concerns.

Dr. Carnine (University of Oregon) testifying to the Senate

▸ "Moving to a response to intervention model can dramatically reduce the long-term failure that is often associated with the IQ-achievement discrepancy formula. 70 to 90 percent of the most at risk children in Kindergarten through 2nd grade can be brought to the average range with effective instruction."

The research into well-implemented RTI or Tiered Intervention has shown that many students who would have previously qualified under SLD have been appropriately served (and have better long term outcomes) through interventions implemented within the general education setting.

Dr. Torgesen from Florida

▸ "Within 1 year following the intervention, 40% of the children were found to be no longer in need of special education services."
▸ This was only 8 weeks of intervention at 2 hours per day and the children were labeled "with severe reading disabilities…"

Whether looking at this research or the research around the Lindamood-Bell approach, it is easy to see that short-term intensive intervention that is focused on the specific needs of the children shows us that many children do not have disabilities, but instead are instructional casualties of our system. The research noted above was with children considered to have "severe reading disabilities." Studies show that similar methods have results of up to 80% of students no longer needing special education services with students who would be considered to have mild reading disabilities. Think about the implications. What if 50% of all students in special education (taking the 80% of SLD students and adding a small error rate in the other categories that are "soft") do not actually have disabilities and actually just need intensive interventions?

WAC 392-172A-03020

"(3) Each school district must ensure that:

(a) Assessments and other evaluation materials used to assess a student:

(i) **Are selected and administered so as not to be discriminatory on a racial or cultural basis;**

(ii) **Are provided and administered in the student's native language or other mode of communication and in the form most likely to yield accurate information** on what the student knows and can do academically, developmentally, and functionally unless it is clearly not feasible to so provide or administer;"

The law states that we are required to have practices that do not lead to discrimination, and that we are required to evaluate in the student's native language (or using a format most likely to yield accurate information). Yet, we know that our practices lead to the use of the SLD category at rates higher for our ELL students (sometimes much higher). And, we are saying that these students have a disability in reading, math or written language in a language they are just learning (unless we have proof that they had the same learning issues in their prior country when applicable).

WAC 392-172A-03040

"(2)(a) A student **must not be determined to be eligible** for special education services **if** the determinant factor is:

> (i) **Lack of appropriate instruction in reading**, based upon the state's grade level standards;

> (ii) **Lack of appropriate instruction in math**; or

> (iii) **Limited English proficiency**; and

(b) If the student does not otherwise meet the eligibility criteria including presence of a disability, adverse educational impact and need for specially designed instruction.

(3) In interpreting evaluation data for the purpose of determining eligibility for special education services, each school district must:

(a) Draw upon information from a variety of sources, including aptitude and achievement tests, parent input, and teacher recommendations, as well as information about the student's physical condition, social or cultural background, and adaptive behavior; and

(b) **Ensure that information obtained from all of these sources is documented and carefully considered**."

Underline added for emphasis.

This law has several issues that apply to evaluation. School teams are supposed to rule-out lack of appropriate instruction in reading and math. However, how does a student get appropriate instruction in reading and math if that instruction is not provided in their native language? School teams are supposed to factor in social and cultural background yet in most evaluations it is very difficult to find evidence of this done with fidelity. Is there appropriate instruction in reading and/or math if less than 50% of the students are passing the state tests? 40%? 30%? 20%?

From the book *English Language Learners with Special Education Needs,* edited by Artiles and Ortiz, written for the Center for Applied Linguistics (it was published in 2002, so some terminology has changed):

▶ "In fact, data suggest that testing English Language Learners in the native language produces unexplained outcomes. In effect, using assessments normed in either the native language or in English with English Language Learners may produce diagnoses that cannot be defended."

These quotes clearly document the concern that using standardized tests on groups of students who do not match the normative group lead to results that just cannot be consistently considered valid.

From Ochoa's and Ortiz's Book Assessing Culturally and Linguistically Diverse Students, page 167.

▶ "It is no doubt apparent at this point that assessment of culturally and linguistically diverse individuals is far more complicated than it may seem on the surface and certainly involves a great deal more than the misguided search for the "right" test."
▶ "School districts that do not have RTI systems in place are 3 times more likely to qualify ELL students for special education than district who have RTI (tiered intervention) systems in place."

Again, looking for the right or magical test is "misguided." Then, contrast that search with the results of districts who are (or are not) using systematic intervention protocols.

The issues within SLD are the most problematic issues, based upon the results. It is the category with the most disproportionality. All districts that have provided me with access to their data prior to providing district level trainings have had rates of qualification for language learners in this category at a significantly higher rate than SLD is used in general in the category. That is, if a district is using the SLD category for 35% of all qualifications they are often using the SLD category for ELL/SPED qualified students for roughly 45-70% of the ELL/SPED qualified students. It has also been the norm that these students are at the beginning stages of language development, without documentation that learning disabilities existed in the native language. In order for a team to qualify a language learner under this category the team will need to determine that the student who is learning English has a disability in reading, math, or written language in English. This statement is based upon the results, not upon what should be occurring.

You have seen the problems and concerns, now what?

We suggest introspection, examining data, using a process, monitoring the results, and adjusting to meet goals that represent proportionality. This is not about putting fewer kids into special education (if your numbers already make sense), and it is also not about putting more kids in either (we are already over identifying). It is about qualifying the right kids. This is hard to do, unless you and your team work to identify the issues and address them.

Systems level work can include the early intervention as noted by Dr. Carnine, the intense intervention noted by Dr. Torgesen, and parent involvement and education which is often forgotten.

These two categories usually have disproportionality and are at times the "gateway drug" into special education and disproportionality:

- Speech or Language Impairment
- Developmental Delay

Each of these two areas has both similar and unique problem areas. Many of the issues within these two categories are caused by staff members not knowing the history of the student or the characteristics of the language of the student.

Speech or Language Impairment

There are two main areas that create concerns: language (expressive and receptive) and articulation. Within the area of language, there are times in which grammar becomes an issue. This tends to ignore the information that exists on the development of language for a second or later language for the student. Even for students who are simultaneous bilinguals, usually one of the languages is not as strong as the other language and will continue to have some grammar issues, possibly throughout life. For students who are sequential bilinguals, mastering certain aspects of grammar may take a lifetime or just may not occur at all. For anyone who is learning Spanish, reaching a near 100% correct usage of "por" y "para" just may never occur. For someone coming from Spanish to English, mastering when to use "in" versus "on" can take a lifetime. I am using the English and Spanish examples given my experience with them, but also because 75% of our ELLs are Spanish to English learners (at last check this was 67% in Washington, and 85% in California).

When an SLP is considering a student for qualification in the category of Speech or Language Impairment, they need to have a strong knowledge of the student's language acquisition history and knowledge about that language within the community. In Steve's experience across many districts, a certain pattern occurs: not all of the languages are represented within the special education student group, and for some languages, students are only qualified in those "hard" categories. For example, the Kent School District normally has 130 to 140 languages spoken. However, we usually only have 40-45 of those languages represented within our special education student population. This is, in part, due to sample sizes (some of the languages only have 1-2 speakers and you should not expect to see a student within all of those groups).

However, that does not explain the size of the difference. Also, some languages are over-represented and the patterns of the over-representation are consistent. Spanish tends to be over represented for language (expressive and receptive) and some Asian languages are over represented for articulation. So, once a therapist knows this information, they can then talk to people about the usage of the language in the community (especially for the high incidence languages). A key issue is whether or not the student in question for qualification for language services actually needs English when they leave the school setting (or even needs it within the school setting). For example, can the student travel within the school or community and only use very little English? If this is the case, then the apparent needs/adverse impact of the student in English would need to be extreme to justify qualification, and the student would need to demonstrate significant issues within their native language (according to multiple speakers of that language). Without this, we would be qualifying students simply because they do not practice something that really is not that important in their life: English. Additionally, their exposure might be limited within and outside the school.

What about articulation? The therapist really needs to know about the structure of the language, whether or not the sounds of English are present within the language of the student, and the developmental norms for that language. It is inappropriate to qualify a student for articulation issues when the sounds that are creating the problematic score do not exist in the primary language of the student or are not yet developmentally expected in the student's native language.

The following charts are used by SLPs to help parents understand the developmental ages related to sounds/blends, the first chart is for English and the second for Spanish. Trying to find this same information for other languages becomes more difficult as the languages become less commonly used. And, we have over 400 languages spoken in our schools in the United States. It takes work to find out the developmentally appropriate ages and the differences in sounds across these 400+ languages, but that is needed to know whether or not your evaluation of the student has any validity or usefulness.

As noted earlier in this book, our tests are not normed in such a way that we can know for sure whether or not the score we are obtaining is meaningful. That is, if the student has been exposed to a very limited range of vocabulary within their environment and scores poorly on our test(s), is that meaningful? It could be that this child is effectively using 90% of the vocabulary they were exposed to, but they were only exposed to 50% of the words compared to the children who the test was normed upon.

English

Developmental Articulation Norms –

AGES

4	5	7	7.5	8.5
m	k	v	r	z
h	g	-ing	l	th (the)
n	d		s	th (with)
w	f		ch	
b	y		sh	
p	t		j	
			/r/ blends	
			/s/ blends	
			/l/ blends	

Based on: Massachusetts Speech and Hearing Association Entrance and Exit Criteria Guidelines
90% mastery

Spanish

Developmental Articulation Norms –

AGES

3	4	5	6	7
m	k	d	x	rr
b	l	g	s	
p	w	ñ		
	f	r		
	y	ch		
	t			
	n			

Based on: Jimenez 1987, Acevedo 1993
90% mastery

At this point, the team has analyzed the student's native language and analyzed issues related to siblings, educational history, environment, etcetera, and determined that the presenting problem would exist if the student was not a language learner. For example, there is evidence that the concerns exist in the student's primary language (and English as applicable), the siblings do not have the same issues, and the student's environment is such that learning English is valued. Then, the SLP must determine if these documented issues reach the level that, if the student were not a language learner, special education eligibility would be the likely decision. If the answer is no, the team needs to understand that language acquisition is the primary factor and speech or language delays are a secondary factor and that would not meet eligibility criteria.

If the team does not have documentation of the developmental norms for the language the student speaks, how would the team know whether or not the "problem" they are seeing is or is not actually a developmentally appropriate expectation within that language? My guess is that almost no one would guess that the rolled "r" in Spanish is not developmentally expected until age seven.

Developmental Delay

The category Developmental Delay consists of five subcategories: Social or Emotional, Adaptive, Communication, Cognitive and Motor (Physical Development).

This category could be the category in which exposure/experience/expectations/practice are the most critical. You will be trying to determine whether or not a young child/student who could be coming to you from poverty with language differences, and probably cultural differences, has a disability that impacts their access to their general daily activities. The Preschool Version of the ELL Critical Data Process focuses on understanding these issues for preschool age language learners. In the end, your team will need to determine whether or not, regardless of the score, the student had a real opportunity to grow the skill in question like a student who was within the normative sample. Remember that the category Developmental Delay is a category of special education. Therefore, the team may indicate a belief that the student is likely to have a disability, which may be accurate, or that the delay may respond to intervention (meaning no disability).

This tends to revolve around issues that are related to social-emotional, adaptive behavior and/or communication. The team, during the ELL Critical Data Process Preschool Version had the responsibility to take these areas into consideration, especially with regards to exposure, experience, expectations and practice. The preschool version is to be used when students have not yet been in school or early in their first year.

A child cannot be qualified as disabled simply because a family cannot or will not create the needed experiences, exposure, expectations and then support these with practice. When the presenting problem does not represent a disability, the problem is better solved through working with the families or communities to create the needed experiences, exposure, expectations and practice. This is not a value judgment. Many families are doing their very best to provide food and shelter.

<u>Exposure, Experience, Expectations and Practice must be examined.</u>

Social/emotional issues: The team must integrate their information from before (or possibly during the referral process) with their data obtained during the evaluation process if an evaluation is recommended and completed. Based on that information, can the team state that social-emotional issues exist to the extent that, after subtracting out issues with exposure/experience/ expectations/ and/or practice, there would still be a large enough problem/concern?

Adaptive behavior: When the team is looking at adaptive behavior, they must go through a similar process, answering the same basic questions. Additionally, they must be able to come to the conclusion that, after subtracting out language and culture (if there are applicable issues), the student would still have significant impacts within adaptive behavior that are directly, or primarily, related to a potential disability. A major hurdle for teams to overcome during this process is the belief that they must provide special education as the early intervention. The issue or problem here is that they are stating that the child has a disability. They are not stating on the report, under qualification, that they "just want to help."

The categories that have had historical problems, yet are showing less disproportionality than other noted categories:

The eligibility categories in this group are difficult to analyze yet are not as extreme as SLI, DD, or SLD. These categories are difficult in this context due to both the impacts of language learning and acculturation issues. Additionally, historical issues of over-qualification of language learners within intellectual disability might have impacted the way in which educators think about this category (i.e., some people might believe that certain groups have higher rates of intellectual disabilities).

- Intellectual Disability
- Emotional Behavioral Disability
- Other Health Impairment

Each of these categories has its own unique issues and problems, with the first category often having had historical over-qualification and the second having both under and over qualification depending upon regional issues and third category having historical under-qualification (under usage of this category, yet possibly putting these children into the SLD category incorrectly).

Intellectual Disability

Qualification for students who are language learners was an extreme problem for many years and is still a problem in some areas of the country. My great-grandfather immigrated through Ellis Island during the period of time when many individuals who did not speak English were labelled as "retarded." Court cases, many of which were in California and Texas, led to much more caution in this area. Today, at least in Washington State, it is rarer to see an ELL student incorrectly qualified in this category. Sadly, when teams do not know what to do, they may default to pushing these hard to identify students into the Specific Learning Disability category through inappropriate application of the legal concept "professional judgment." If your team is facing this tough decision, there are ways to look at the data and come to a better decision.

The team will need intellectual test data and adaptive behavior score data. As noted before, for language learners these are both very problematic areas to measure with our current tests. Therefore, the team needs to spend a greater portion of the time on documenting other sources of information that either defend or negate the standardized test measures. The ELL Critical Data Process will provide some of this information, yet the team needs to put the puzzle pieces together. Also, if a team is travelling down this "road" they need to ask more questions. It is very important to understand how the student functions in many different environments, especially when the environment is supported by their native language.

Examples:

At home, church, and/or other family activities, how does this child compare to other children? Do they understand the games being played at the level other children do? Can they be given the same types of chores the other children are given? If age appropriate, can they independently walk around their community (find their way at an age appropriate level)? What are the games and hobbies they have and are these age appropriate?

Teams often default to non-verbal IQ testing and trust those results without question. However, that ignores the fact that the test was normed on a group of children who had much different life experiences than the child you might be testing. Non-verbal IQ tests rely heavily on understanding how to analyze patterns and choose pictorial representations that may complete these patterns. Therefore, children who grew up with access to certain toys (Legos, Lincoln Logs, Erector Sets, puzzles, etcetera) and who had access to certain books (e.g., Where is Waldo?) have an enormous advantage on non-verbal IQ tests.

If you must use a non-verbal IQ test (which is virtually always better than an IQ test that has verbal portions for a person who does not speak English), then you need to watch for patterns. For example, the C-TONI series has 6 subtests. When testing a student who has a very different background than the normative group, you might see the following: you begin the testing and the student is doing terribly, then, near the end of the second or the beginning of the third subtest you "see the lightbulb come on" and the student's performance increases dramatically. You can then, in many cases, use the average of the later subtests to represent the student's real performance on this test. In all likelihood it is still an underestimation (given not enough practice), but it will show you a much different perspective on the student's intellectual ability.

The second problem area is adaptive behavior assessment (the second required area for the category of intellectual disability). During this area of assessment you are going to be asking a family who likely does not speak English to answer questions that can make them very uncomfortable. In addition, these scales are normed on what we believe is appropriate development in these areas (given the normative sample). In many cases you will get results that are totally useless or of such questionable use that you cannot make a determination from this information. Therefore, if you must use an adaptive behavior measure, you really need to get to know more about the exposure and experiences of the student. For example, for a student who is unable to feed themselves (according to the rating scale), have they ever been asked/required to do so? Or, for a student who cannot put on a jacket by themselves, did they live in an area in which the weather didn't require the use of jackets? Or, for a student who cannot tie their own shoes, do they have shoes without laces? Keep going with this line of logic for any question in which a student is not demonstrating a skill, just in case they had limited exposure/experience/practice.

Then, start asking about the daily life of the student in their previous environment. It is possible you are going to find out that they can do something rather difficult that many people "here" could not do (e.g., start a fire without matches, hunt/fish with limited resources, etcetera). In the end, you must take into account the relationship of exposure/experience/practice to actual performance. It is unfair to consider a student impaired for something they have never had exposure/experience/practice with, or that it was very limited. For example, considering a student to have fine motor issues with a pencil when they only just started to use one. Also, it would be unfair to neglect the skills a student has that are not measured on our rating scales. In the end, though, the team will need to make a determination based on exposure/experience/practice: does this student actually have an impairment or not?

Emotional Behavioral Disability

Within my experiences in the state of Washington, I have rarely seen this category as problematic for over-identification. People from other regions of the country have reported over qualification in this category.

It has been notable for significant under-identification when compared to all students in special education, here in Washington. The problem is, for me, I have yet to see any research or evidence to point to the under-identification actually being "real." Many of the students who are identified within this category who are not ELL students tend to be students with some form of social maladjustment. They are in environments that are very problematic and their interactions with the world represent a series of learned behaviors. Also, rarely seen in this category are the students whose mental health issues are internalizing by nature. In other words, if the behavior negatively impacts the adults, we tend to qualify the students and if the behavior negatively impacts the students "in a quiet way" we tend to not qualify the students. Therefore, it is hard to know for sure whether or not an underrepresentation of ELL students is meaningful.

In order to make this decision, you need to be able to rule-out a lot of issues.

First, is the student's "bad" behavior (we would not be looking at this category if bad behavior was not present) actually the cause of the adverse impact on their access to their education? Or, is the lack of ability to communicate needs and wants creating bad behavior (due to frustration)? You are only going to be able to analyze this if you have the data very well documented for your school and district. In other words, how many of your ELL students are demonstrating problem behaviors and to what degree? What percentage of your ELL students are finding academic success? How does that rate compare to research on effective ELL programs (look into the work of Dr. Collier and Dr. Thomas, if you have not already done so).

Second, is the student a student who needs support for trauma? If there is a history of trauma, and it is untreated, you could begin to provide support for the student that is of little or no value.

Third, what is the relationship of academic struggles to the noted behavior? That is, if a student is behaving poorly to hide academic struggles then the intervention needed is much different than if the bad behaviors are causing academic struggles.

Last, is there a cultural issue that is not being addressed? The majority of students qualified in this category are boys and some of our boys are coming from cultures that have a very different outlook in general and sometimes specifically in male/female power relationships. This is a difficult area to address, but we do not want to label a child as disabled due to struggles they are having with cultural differences.

If the team can document that the behaviors and/or emotions are the cause of the adverse impact on the student accessing their education, and that this would be occurring with or without the impact of being a language learner, then the team needs to understand the behaviors at a deeper level. The goal in the end is to teach the student new skills, and/or behaviors, to get their needs met. Therefore, understanding the root cause of the behaviors and how language learning plays into each behavior is critical in the development of interventions, whether in special education or not.

Other Health Impairment

The issue here tends to be under qualification. In many cases, this appears to be caused by the difficulties the families face in navigating our medical system. These struggles often lead to under identification in this category. And, from what I have seen from many districts, the students who are struggling are then placed into the Specific Learning Disability category.

The category Other Health Impairment tends to be easier in the terms of qualification, if one can get the needed documentation. It is important to note that the laws place the responsibility on the district, at no cost to the parents, to obtain any information that it believes necessary to appropriately qualify a student. That is a very tricky responsibility to navigate and staff really need to work with their administrative teams to travel that road.

If you have the needed documentation, the process is reasonably simple. In any of these cases, the team needs to determine the relationship between the noted condition, the adverse impact to accessing their education (with and without language impact) and whether or not the student needs specially designed instruction in order to access their education that is not dependent upon impacts of language acquisition. If language learning was not an issue, would the medical condition by itself be creating this adverse impact? To the same extent?

The issue here, quite often for our families, is navigating the medical system. At this point, you have completed the ELL Critical Data Process and have a document from a medical provider (or other if your state law allows) that documents a medical condition. The team must now decide whether or not that medical condition is the cause (or primary cause) of the noted adverse impact. This needs to be documented such that any reasonable person reading it can follow the logic as to how the medical condition is or is not related to the adverse impact on the student accessing their education. Then, if the team decides that the medical condition is the cause (or primary cause) of the adverse impact, the team needs to determine if the student needs specially designed instruction to address the issues. What new skills would the student be taught in order to "work around" the impact of the medical condition to better or fully access their education? If an accommodation or modification addresses the issue, then the student is not eligible. For example, if assistive technology alone allows the student to access their education without an adverse impact, then the student is not eligible for special education services.

The eligibility categories with the least disproportionality:

By any chance, are we evaluating a student who happens to possibly be eligible in one of the "hard" categories? The "hard" categories are more concrete in nature and it is likely that language acquisition is not a determinant factor.

- Hearing Impairment or Deafness
- Visual Impairment (including Blindness)
- Orthopedic Impairment
- Traumatic Brain Injury
- Deaf-Blind
- Multiple Disabilities
- Autism

Hearing Impairment or Deafness

We will start out by pointing out the obvious: the team needs documentation that the student either has a Hearing Impairment or Deafness as defined by their state laws. Then, the team needs to consider the adverse impact on the student's access to their education. When doing this, the team needs to discuss the extent to which language acquisition is adding to the observed adverse impact. If the student was not an English Language Learner, would we be discussing only accommodations and modification (in other words, a 504 plan)?

It is likely that any student brought up to the team with documented hearing issues believed to be the cause of noted adverse impacts will qualify for either a 504 plan or for Special Education Services. The dividing line is whether accommodations/modifications with appropriate (research proven) ELL services would meet the needs of the student versus the documented need for specially designed instruction (which indicates Special Education Qualification is appropriate).

Visual Impairment (Including Blindness)

For this category, too, the team needs documentation that the student has either a Visual Impairment or Blindness as defined by their state laws. Then, the team needs to consider the adverse impact on the student's access to their education. When doing this, the team needs to discuss the extent to which language acquisition is adding to the observed adverse impact. If the student was not an English Language Learner, would we be discussing only accommodations and modification (in other words, a 504 plan)?

It is likely that any student brought up to the team with documented vision issues believed to be the cause of noted adverse impacts will qualify for either a 504 plan or for Special Education Services. The dividing line is whether accommodations/modifications with appropriate (research proven) ELL services would meet the needs of the student versus the documented need for specially designed instruction (which indicates Special Education Qualification is appropriate).

Orthopedic Impairment

Again, the team needs documentation that the student has an Orthopedic Impairment as defined by their state laws. Then, the team needs to consider the adverse impact on the student's access to their education. When doing this, the team needs to discuss the extent to which language acquisition is adding to the observed adverse impact. If the student was not an English Language Learner, would we be discussing only accommodations and modification (in other words, a 504 plan)? It is likely that any student brought up to the team with documented orthopedic issues believed to be the cause of noted adverse impacts will qualify for either a 504 plan or for Special Education Services.

The dividing line is whether accommodations/modifications with appropriate (research proven) ELL services would meet the needs of the student versus the documented need for specially designed instruction (which indicates Special Education Qualification is appropriate).

It is important to note that staff will often want more services for students who struggle physically than the student may need. In many cases, these students simply need accommodations and/or modifications given their physical challenges. The world has benefitted greatly from seeing Steven Hawking as an example of a person whose mind was not impacted by the struggles of his body.

Traumatic Brain Injury

As with the previous categories, the team needs to document that the student has a Traumatic Brain Injury (TBI) as defined by their state laws. The problems arise in this area not so much as whether a student needs help, but instead that many people incorrectly use this category in place of Other Health Impairment. This category is solely for students whose brain damage is based upon a trauma/injury (some states have changed their interpretation of this area, so make sure to check your state laws). Many students enter this category based upon being hit by a car and this category is not for events like strokes (strokes, in most states, would fall under the category of Other Health Impairment). Then, the team needs to consider the adverse impact on the student's access to their education. When doing this, the team needs to discuss the extent to which language acquisition is adding to the observed adverse impact. If the student was not an English Language Learner, would we be discussing only accommodations and modification (in other words, a 504 plan)? It is likely that any student brought up to the team with a documented TBI is going to qualify for special education services. Nevertheless, the team does need to keep an open mind to the options.

Deaf-Blind

We will start out by pointing out the obvious: the team needs documentation that the student has both Deafness and Blindness as defined by their state laws (I have yet to see anyone get this category wrong). Then, the team needs to consider the adverse impact on the student's access to their education. When doing this, the team needs to discuss the extent to which language acquisition is adding to the observed adverse impact. If the student was not an English Language Learner, would we be discussing only accommodations and modification (in other words, a 504 plan)?

It is likely that any student brought up to the team with documented hearing and vision issues believed to be the cause of noted adverse impacts will qualify for either a 504 plan or for Special Education Services. The dividing line is whether accommodations/modifications with appropriate (research proven) ELL services would meet the needs of the student versus the documented need for specially designed instruction (which indicates Special Education

Qualification is appropriate). In practice, the vast majority of the students who fit into this category need special education services and a lack of English acquisition is not a determining factor.

Multiple Disabilities

In this case, the practitioner really needs to understand the state laws under which they operate. In our experience, most times there is an indication that the student would independently qualify in two or more of the categories as listed in the CFR creating the "multiple." Additionally, many states indicate that the severity needs to be such that the student's needs cannot be met by using just one category or the other. A common mistake is the use of two medical diagnosis that actually fit under the same category to create the "multi" eligibility. The good news is that this category is rarely used for students who do not actually need special education services, and most errors are related to using this category in place of Other Health Impairment, Intellectually Disabled, or Orthopedic Impairment when the criteria for "multi" has not actually been met. Therefore, the team needs to use the information required within two or more other categories (never Deaf-Blind and virtually never Specific Learning Disability) to determine whether the child meets two or more categories. Then, depending upon state law in your area, the team may need to meet an additional criteria as noted above.

Autism

We will start out, again, by pointing out the obvious. As always, the team needs documentation that the student has a diagnosis of Autism (or related disorder depending upon your state special education laws). Make sure to check for updates in this area, given it has been changing greatly in recent years (written in 2018). The laws sometimes indicate the type or range of practitioner who can provide this diagnosis. Then, the team needs to consider the adverse impact on the student's access to their education. When doing this, the team needs to discuss the extent to which language acquisition is adding to the observed adverse impact. If the student was not an English Language Learner, would we be discussing only accommodations and modification (in other words, a 504 plan)? It is likely that any student brought up to the team with documented Autism Spectrum Disorder issues believed to be the cause of noted adverse impacts will qualify for either a 504 plan or for special education services. The dividing line is whether accommodations/modifications with appropriate (research proven) ELL services would meet the needs of the student versus the documented need for specially designed instruction (which indicates special education qualification is appropriate).

Standardized testing

Depending upon your state, you may or may not be required to complete standardized testing. Standardized testing gets demonized, yet the issue is not actually with the tests. The problem occurs when the tests are used incorrectly or when the information is incorrectly analyzed and/or applied. A standardized reading test in English that demonstrates that a student cannot read in English is in all likelihood correct. However, it does not demonstrate whether or not they can read in any other language (or at what level). Also, for students who have been in the United States for a few years, interpreting and generalizing the information is very difficult. The question is, what is reasonable growth per year in reading in English, when you are just learning English? Also, what if the student did not learn to read in their primary language? What if the student did? How do each of these scenarios impact the expected or reasonable rates of learning to read in English (knowing the first group of students does not have transferable skills)?

Using standardized tests is perfectly fine, if you have clear goals for the information and understand the limitations. A reasonable use for these tests is to set a baseline to compare against at a later time. However, that later comparison is meaningless if the student is not receiving a form of education that is proven to be effective for language learners. The following quote repeated from earlier (this time in expanded form), is critical to remember when testing involves standardized tests:

From the book, *English Language Learners with Special Education Needs* (edited by Artiles and Ortiz, written for the Center for Applied Linguistics). It was published in 2002, so some terminology has changed.

▸ "A critical assumption of many test makers and users is that it is possible to test an English Language Learner as long as the same test is available in the learner's first and second language. Typically, such tests have norms for each language. Monolingual norms may not be appropriate for a child in the process of becoming bilingual, however (Grosjean, 1989). In fact, data suggest that testing English Language Learners in the native language produces unexplained outcomes. In an important study that used psychometric tests developed for Spanish Speakers, Rueda and his colleagues (Rueda, Figueroa, Mercado, & Cardoza, 1984) found that English Language Learners who had not been referred for special education, the test misdiagnosed 47% with learning disabilities and 7% with mental retardation. Among those students diagnosed by the school system as learning disabled, and a diagnosis of mental retardation was confirmed for only 58% of the English Language Learners placed in programs for students with mental retardation. In effect, using assessments normed in either the native language or in English with English Language Learners may produce diagnoses that cannot be defended."

▸ "Too often, however, the hope that special education will close achievement gaps is not realized. For example, reevaluations of Hispanic students who had been in special education for 3 years showed that their IQ scores were lower than at initial placement and that their achievement scores were essentially the same as at entry (Wilkinson &

Ortiz, 1986). This is disturbing given the likelihood that some of these youngsters were actually Type I or Type II students, neither general education nor special education met their needs."

The book describes, in a nutshell, Type I students as those who fail due to systems issues, Type II students who fail due to non-systems issues, and Type III students as those who truly have disabilities.

Therefore, before even using standardized testing, the team needs to discuss what they hope to learn from the standardized testing for this individual student. And someone on the team needs to speak to whether or not that is a feasible expectation, given what tests are available and how they have been normed.

Appendix A: Face Validity

Face Validity is being used in this context to indicate whether or not a person who is trained in evaluating students for special education could look at the evaluation report, and, after a quick first the read of report, would conclude the qualification appears to be valid. This person would not know the student personally, but upon reading the report would believe that the team had completed a thoughtful and thorough process that is solidly based upon data documented in the report.

In this appendix, the authors are providing charts for each of the eligibility categories to help the team document whether or not they have documented a case for eligibility and how strong that case is for eligibility. Each of these are on their own page so that you can make copies as needed. The description includes a list of Face Validity items that apply to all students who are evaluated and also ELL specific requirements.

Please note, many of the categories that are first listed are "hard" categories and the questions under the "Language Learning" section are going to be very similar. This is in part related to why these are considered "hard" categories and in part related to why there is very little disproportionality in these categories. In other words, we almost always get these categories correct, even for our language learners. The later categories have more significant differences.

There will be areas in which the team will be asked to write something that passes the "stranger test." This is referring to the ability to write a rationale such that anyone who is a stranger to the student and situation could read what the team has written and understand the reasoning. So, could a stranger read your report and understand why your team made the decisions that were made?

The team needs to complete the chart by stating Yes or No to each of the Face Validity items and language acquisition items. If a Face Validity item is missing, the team needs to complete that item before making an eligibility decision. If the answer is "yes" to a language learner issue, the team then needs to be able to document and articulate how language learning was not the primary factor and that the problem would have existed even if language learning was not a factor.

Your state may have additional criteria that you would need to add to the checklist. It is your responsibility to determine if additional requirements need to be met. Also, in all cases, your district can choose to add criteria where additions make sense to your teams.

The ELL Critical Data Process can be done more quickly with the "hard" categories and at times not completed for the "hard" categories when the disability is clear and obvious. For example, a student who is medically fragile and has a very limited vocabulary in their native language.

EXAMPLE CHECKLIST

Each section will have a chart like the following chart (often with fewer items). The column on the left is whether or not the Face Validity item is present and the column on the right is whether or not language learning is a factor for that item.

	Evidence Documented?			Language Impact?	
	Yes	No		Yes	No
1)	____	____		____	____
2)	____	____		____	____
3)	____	____		____	____
4)	____	____		____	____
5)	____	____		____	____
6)	____	____		____	____
7)	____	____		____	____
8)	____	____		____	____
9)	____	____		____	____
10)	____	____		____	____

Important

Before the evaluation, ensure that the following were completed:

- The ELL Critical Data Process was completed by the team and the team agreed that a special education evaluation was needed.
- School data has been evaluated and processed to show impact (or lack thereof) of school practices on qualification rates of language learners.

Any time you make a decision regarding a Yes/No question, it is critically important to make sure that decision is not being impacted by social pressures and/or wants of specific team members. In other words, do not get pressured into bad decisions (e.g., special education is the only resource). Begin and end decision making with data.

Hearing Impairment Form

Obtain or document during the evaluation process:

Face Validity:

1) Documentation of a hearing impairment or fluctuating hearing from a qualified provider.
2) Testing or measurement in all areas of proposed qualification.
3) General education input that is supportive of qualification.
4) Explanation and description of adverse impact and need for specially designed instruction (SDI) as related to this specific data.

> **Before the evaluation, ensure that the following were completed:**
>
> 1. The ELL Critical Data Process was completed by the team and the team agreed that a special education evaluation was needed.
> 2. School data has been evaluated and processed to show impact (or lack thereof) of school practices on qualification rates of language learners.

Language Learning:

5) Documentation of impact of language learning on hearing testing (Did the student fully understand the directions? If no, check yes for language impact).
6) For adverse impact, documentation of how language learning and hearing are each separately related to the adverse impact (both in the classroom and the testing).

Checklist to Meet a Minimum Standard for Hearing Impairment

	Evidence Documented?			Language Impact?	
	Yes	No		Yes	No
1)	____	____		____	____
2)	____	____		____	____
3)	____	____		____	____
4)	____	____		____	____
5)	____	____		____	____
6)	____	____		____	____

> As noted earlier in the book, in these cases language acquisition is usually an additional factor yet not a determining factor. Whether or not they were a language learner, they would have needs that would need to be addressed from either special education or a 504 plan.

Narrative for any items answered yes in column 3:

Deafness Form

Obtain or document during the evaluation process:

Face Validity:

<table>
<tr><td></td><td>

Before the evaluation, ensure that the following were completed:

1. The ELL Critical Data Process was completed by the team and the team agreed that a special education evaluation was needed.
2. School data has been evaluated and processed to show impact (or lack thereof) of school practices on qualification rates of language learners.

</td></tr>
</table>

Face Validity:

1) Documentation from a qualified provider that the student has deafness.
2) Testing or measurement in all areas of proposed qualification.
3) General education input that is supportive of qualification. If not possible, documented explanation.
4) Explanation and description of adverse impact and need for specially designed instruction (SDI) as related to this specific data.

Language Learning:

5) Documentation of impact of language learning on hearing testing (Did the student fully understand the directions? If no, check yes for language impact).
6) For adverse impact, documentation of how language learning and hearing are each separately related to the adverse impact (both test scores and classroom data).

Checklist to Meet a Minimum Standard for Deafness

	Evidence Documented?		Language Impact?	
	Yes	No	Yes	No
1)	_____	_____	_____	_____
2)	_____	_____	_____	_____
3)	_____	_____	_____	_____
4)	_____	_____	_____	_____
5)	_____	_____	_____	_____
6)	_____	_____	_____	_____

As noted earlier in the book, in these cases language acquisition is usually an additional factor yet not a determining factor. Whether or not they were a language learner, they would have needs that would need to be addressed from either special education or a 504 plan.

Narrative for any items answered yes in column 3:

Visual Impairment (Including Blindness) Form

Obtain or document during the evaluation process:

Face Validity:

1) Documentation from a qualified provider that the student has a visual impairment or blindness.
2) Testing or measurement in all areas of proposed qualification.
3) General education input that is supportive of qualification.
4) Explanation and description of adverse impact and need for specially designed instruction (SDI) as related to this specific data.

Before the evaluation, ensure that the following were completed:

1. The ELL Critical Data Process was completed by the team and the team agreed that a special education evaluation was needed.
2. School data has been evaluated and processed to show impact (or lack thereof) of school practices on qualification rates of language learners.

Language Learning:

5) Documentation of impact of language learning on vision testing (Did the student fully understand the directions? If no, check yes for language impact.).
6) For adverse impact, documentation of how language learning and vision are each separately related to the adverse impact (both classroom and testing data).

Checklist to Meet a Minimum Standard for Visual Impairment (Including Blindness)

	Evidence Documented?		Language Impact?	
	Yes	No	Yes	No
1)	____	____	____	____
2)	____	____	____	____
3)	____	____	____	____
4)	____	____	____	____
5)	____	____	____	____
6)	____	____	____	____

Narrative for any items answered yes in column 3:

As noted earlier in the book, in these cases language acquisition is usually an additional factor yet not a determining factor. Whether or not they were a language learner, they would have needs that would need to be addressed from either special education or a 504 plan.

Orthopedic Impairment Form

Obtain or document during the evaluation process:

Before the evaluation, ensure that the following were completed:

1. The ELL Critical Data Process was completed by the team and the team agreed that a special education evaluation was needed.
2. School data has been evaluated and processed to show impact (or lack thereof) of school practices on qualification rates of language learners.

Face Validity:

1) Documentation of a related medical condition that meets the WAC (or your state) criteria by a qualified provider.
2) Testing and/or measurement in all areas of proposed qualification.
3) General education input that is supportive of qualification.
4) Specially designed instruction (SDI) includes services from an OT and/or PT.
5) Explanation and description of adverse impact and need for SDI as related to this specific data.

Language Learning:

6) Documentation of impact of language learning on motor testing (Did the student fully understand the directions? If no, check yes for language impact).
7) For adverse impact, documentation of how language learning and physical restrictions created by the orthopedic issues are each separately related to the adverse impact.

Checklist to Meet a Minimum Standard for Orthopedic Impairment

	Evidence Documented?			Language Impact?	
	Yes	No		Yes	No
1)	___	___		___	___
2)	___	___		___	___
3)	___	___		___	___
4)	___	___		___	___
5)	___	___		___	___
6)	___	___		___	___
7)	___	___		___	___

As noted earlier in the book, in these cases language acquisition is usually an additional factor yet not a determining factor. Whether or not they were a language learner, they would have needs that would need to be addressed from either special education or a 504 plan.

Narrative for any items answered yes in column 3:

Traumatic Brain Injury Form

Obtain or document during the evaluation process:

Face Validity:

1) Documentation of an injury, from a qualified practitioner, that meets the WAC (or your state) criteria.
2) Testing or measurement in all areas of proposed qualification.
3) General education input that is supportive of qualification.
4) Explanation and description of adverse impact and need for specially designed instruction (SDI) as related to this specific data.

Language Learning:

5) Documentation of impact of language learning on all testing (Did the student fully understand the directions? If no, check yes for language impact).
6) For adverse impact, documentation of how language learning and the brain injury are each separately related to the adverse impact (the team needs information regarding the student's functioning before and after the trauma).

<table>
<tr><td>Before the evaluation, ensure that the following were completed:</td></tr>
</table>

1. The ELL Critical Data Process was completed by the team and the team agreed that a special education evaluation was needed.
2. School data has been evaluated and processed to show impact (or lack thereof) of school practices on qualification rates of language learners.

Checklist to Meet a Minimum Standard for Traumatic Brain Injury

	Evidence Documented?		Language Impact?	
	Yes	No	Yes	No
1)	___	___	___	___
2)	___	___	___	___
3)	___	___	___	___
4)	___	___	___	___
5)	___	___	___	___
6)	___	___	___	___

Narrative for any items answered yes in column 3:

As noted earlier in the book, in these cases language acquisition is usually an additional factor yet not a determining factor. Whether or not they were a language learner, they would have needs that would need to be addressed from either special education or a 504 plan.

Deaf-Blind Form

Obtain or document during the evaluation process:

Face Validity:

1) Documentation from a qualified provider that the student has deafness and blindness.
2) Testing or measurement in all areas of proposed qualification.
3) If available, general education input that is supportive of qualification (if not available, explain why it is not available).
4) Explanation and description of adverse impact and need for specially designed instruction (SDI) as related to this specific data.

Language Learning:

5) Documentation of impact of language on vision and hearing testing (Did the student fully understand the directions? If no, check yes for language impact).
6) For adverse impact, documentation of how language learning and vision/hearing are each separately related to the adverse impact.

Before the evaluation, ensure that the following were completed:

1. The ELL Critical Data Process was completed by the team and the team agreed that a special education evaluation was needed.
2. School data has been evaluated and processed to show impact (or lack thereof) of school practices on qualification rates of language learners.

Checklist to Meet the Standard for Deaf/Blind

	Evidence Documented?		Language Impact?	
	Yes	No	Yes	No
1)	_____	_____	_____	_____
2)	_____	_____	_____	_____
3)	_____	_____	_____	_____
4)	_____	_____	_____	_____
5)	_____	_____	_____	_____
6)	_____	_____	_____	_____

As noted earlier in the book, in these cases language acquisition is usually an additional factor yet not a determining factor. Whether or not they were a language learner, they would have needs that would need to be addressed from either special education or a 504 plan.

Narrative for any items answered yes in column 3:

Multiple Disabilities Form

Obtain or document during the evaluation process:

Face Validity:

1) The documentation of two (or more) of the 13 disability categories, using the guidance from your district or state regarding the categories that logically could fit together.
2) These students are usually severely impacted students and are usually in the most restrictive of settings due to their significant needs. Can you document this?
3) A description of how the impairments are "the combination of which causes such severe educational needs that they cannot be accommodated in special education programs solely for one of the impairments." This is WAC (Washington Administrative Code – The Special Education section) wording, you need to examine the wording of your state laws.
4) If available, general education input that is supportive of qualification (if not available, explain why it is not available).
5) Explanation and description of adverse impact and need for specially designed instruction (SDI) as related to this specific data.

> **Before the evaluation, ensure that the following were completed:**
>
> 1. The ELL Critical Data Process was completed by the team and the team agreed that a special education evaluation was needed.
> 2. School data has been evaluated and processed to show impact (or lack thereof) of school practices on qualification rates of language learners.

Language Learning:

6) Documentation of impact of language on all testing (Did the student fully understand the directions? If no, check yes for language impact).
7) For adverse impact, documentation of how language and each disability category are separately related to the adverse impact.

Checklist to Meet the Standard for Multiple Disability

	Evidence Documented?			Language Impact?	
	Yes	No		Yes	No
1)	____	____		____	____
2)	____	____		____	____
3)	____	____		____	____
4)	____	____		____	____
5)	____	____		____	____
6)	____	____		____	____
7)	____	____		____	____

> As noted earlier in the book, in these cases language acquisition is usually an additional factor yet not a determining factor. Whether or not they were a language learner, they would have needs that would need to be addressed from either special education or a 504 plan.

Narrative for any items answered yes in column 3:

Autism Form

Obtain or document during the evaluation process:

Before the evaluation, ensure that the following were completed:

1. The ELL Critical Data Process was completed by the team and the team agreed that a special education evaluation was needed.
2. School data has been evaluated and processed to show impact (or lack thereof) of school practices on qualification rates of language learners.

Face Validity:

1) Documentation from a qualified provider that the student has Autism, Asperger's, PDD or equivalent. Check your state requirements and note the DSM changes and shifts in the related definitions.
2) Test/measurement data in all areas noted as concerns (usually academic, social, behavioral, communication as a minimum).
3) Communication (especially pragmatics) must be addressed, given that this is one of the core diagnostic features in an autism diagnosis. Use caution with tests that average pragmatic language with vocabulary.
4) More extensive observational documentation to assist with understanding the environmental issues impacting the student. Research on students with autism indicates many issues can be solved by changes to the environment and/or rituals within the environment.
5) General education input that is supportive of qualification. If not possible, documented explanation.
6) Explanation and description of adverse impact and need for specially designed instruction (SDI) as related to this specific data.

Language Learning:

7) Documentation of impact of language on all testing (Did the student fully understand the directions? If no, check yes for language impact).
8) For adverse impact, documentation of how language learning and the impacts of Autism are each separately related to the adverse impact.
9) Autism is in many ways a disability of "communication." The team needs to be able to describe the likely impact of the Autism versus the likely impact of language learning. In other words, how would the student function (demonstrate adverse impact and need for SDI) if they were not a language learner?

Checklist to Meet the Standard for Autism

	Evidence Documented?		Language Impact?	
	Yes	No	Yes	No
1)	_____	_____	_____	_____
2)	_____	_____	_____	_____
3)	_____	_____	_____	_____
4)	_____	_____	_____	_____
5)	_____	_____	_____	_____
6)	_____	_____	_____	_____
7)	_____	_____	_____	_____
8)	_____	_____	_____	_____
9)	_____	_____	_____	_____

Narrative for any items answered yes in column 3:

Intellectual Disability Form

Obtain or document during the evaluation process:

Check your state laws regarding number 1 and 2.

Face Validity:

1) Intellectual test data that is <u>approximately</u> a standard score of 70 or below (or -2.0 SDs). Note, students can be qualified with scores slightly higher when the overall data is supportive.
2) Adaptive behavior data that is <u>approximately</u> a standard score of 70 or below (or -2.0 SDs).
3) Academic data that is supportive of an intellectual disability and a need for specially designed instruction (SDI) (this is not a requirement of eligibility, but it's hard to defend a case without this).
4) Areas of SDI should be reflective of a student with an ID (e.g., learning to write a sentence versus learning to write for different audiences).
5) General education input that is supportive of qualification.
6) Explanation and description of adverse impact and need for SDI as related to this specific data.

Language Learning:

7) Documentation of impact of language on all testing (Did the student fully understand the directions? If no, check yes for language impact). The team needs to be able to show, with the integration of multiple sources of data, how language impacts the testing. Can the team clearly state that the scores would be in the ID range if the student was not a language learner?
8) For adverse impact, documentation of how language learning and intellectual functioning are each separately related to the adverse impact.
9) Does the team have evidence that the tests that were chosen have historically worked with the noted language group?
10) Does the team have evidence that the tests that were chosen have historically worked with the noted cultural group? For example, Adaptive Behavior evaluation has many weaknesses when used with students from other countries and/or cultures, given some of the items are measuring skills not expected or practiced.

Checklist to Meet the Standard for Intellectual Disability

	Evidence Documented?		Language Impact?	
	Yes	No	Yes	No
1)	____	____	____	____
2)	____	____	____	____
3)	____	____	____	____
4)	____	____	____	____
5)	____	____	____	____
6)	____	____	____	____
7)	____	____	____	____
8)	____	____	____	____
9)	____	____	____	____
10)	____	____	____	____

Narrative for any items answered yes in column 3:

Emotional Behavioral Disability Form

Obtain or document during the evaluation process:

Before the evaluation, ensure that the following were completed:

1. The ELL Critical Data Process was completed by the team and the team agreed that a special education evaluation was needed.
2. School data has been evaluated and processed to show impact (or lack thereof) of school practices on qualification rates of language learners.

Face Validity:

1) Behavioral ratings that are significantly outside the norm.
2) Documentation of in-school behaviors that are significantly outside the norm (and have occurred over a long period of time).
3) Explanation of how one (or more) of the noted A-E (see WAC- Washington Administrative Code- Special Education Section) are documented using the noted data. Or use your state's language that is based on the federal language.
4) If available, general education input that is supportive of qualification (if not available, explain why it is not available).
5) Explanation and description of adverse impact and need for specially designed instruction (SDI) as related to this specific data.

Language Learning:

6) Documentation of impact of language on all testing (Did the student fully understand the directions? If no, check yes for language impact).
7) For adverse impact, documentation of how language learning and the impacts of EBD are each separately related to the adverse impact.
8) Does the team have evidence of trauma? Some of our language learners are coming from environments in which trauma was common. Trauma can mimic disability in some cases, yet the needed interventions are VERY different. If trauma is present, a great deal of evidence is needed to support a disability beyond what is normally presented.
9) If number 8 was answered "yes," can the team describe (to a stranger) how the noted impacts are or are not related to the impacts of trauma?

Checklist to Meet the Standard for Emotional Behavioral Disability

	Evidence Documented?		Language Impact?	
	Yes	No	Yes	No
1)	_____	_____	_____	_____
2)	_____	_____	_____	_____
3)	_____	_____	_____	_____
4)	_____	_____	_____	_____
5)	_____	_____	_____	_____
6)	_____	_____	_____	_____
7)	_____	_____	_____	_____
8)	_____	_____	_____	_____
9)	_____	_____	_____	_____

Narrative for any items answered yes in column 3:

Other Health Impairment Form

Obtain or document during the evaluation process:

Face Validity:

1) Documentation of a medical condition by a qualified provider.
2) Documentation of an adverse educational impact directly and logically related to the noted medical condition.
3) Test data in area of specially designed instruction (SDI) that is supportive of qualification.
4) General education input that is supportive of qualification.
5) Explanation and description of adverse impact and need for SDI as related to this specific data.

Language Learning:

6) Documentation of impact of language on all testing (Did the student fully understand the directions? If no, check yes for language impact).
7) For adverse impact, documentation of how language learning and the impacts of the documented medical condition are each separately related to the adverse impact.

Before the evaluation, ensure that the following were completed:
1. The ELL Critical Data Process was completed by the team and the team agreed that a special education evaluation was needed.
2. School data has been evaluated and processed to show impact (or lack thereof) of school practices on qualification rates of language learners.

Checklist to Meet the Standard for Other Health Impairment

	Evidence Documented?		Language Impact?	
	Yes	No	Yes	No
1)	_____	_____	_____	_____
2)	_____	_____	_____	_____
3)	_____	_____	_____	_____
4)	_____	_____	_____	_____
5)	_____	_____	_____	_____
6)	_____	_____	_____	_____
7)	_____	_____	_____	_____

Narrative for any items answered yes in column 3:

Speech or Language Impairment

Obtain or document during the evaluation process:

Face Validity:

1) Test/measurement (formal and informal) data in the area(s) of qualification.
2) Information from the general education setting that includes specific examples of area of qualification that support decision. Or, for preschool children, from appropriate activities.
3) Rule out cultural and "second" language issues.
4) Limitations of testing has been documented in direct relationship to this individual student's situation.
5) Explanation and description of adverse impact and need for specially designed instruction (SDI) as related to this specific data.

Language Learning:

6) Documentation of impact of language on all testing (Did the student fully understand the directions? If no, check yes for language impact).
7) Has the team documented the impact of sequential or simultaneous bilingual impact on the presenting problems?
8) For adverse impact, documentation of how language learning and the impacts of the speech or language impairment are each separately related to the adverse impact.

Before the evaluation, ensure that the following were completed:

1) The ELL Critical Data Process was completed by the team and the team agreed that a special education evaluation was needed.
2) School data has been evaluated and processed to show impact (or lack thereof) of school practices on qualification rates of language learners.

Checklist to Meet the Standard for Speech or Language Impairment

	Evidence Documented?		Language Impact?	
	Yes	No	Yes	No
1)	_____	_____	_____	_____
2)	_____	_____	_____	_____
3)	_____	_____	_____	_____
4)	_____	_____	_____	_____
5)	_____	_____	_____	_____
6)	_____	_____	_____	_____
7)	_____	_____	_____	_____
8)	_____	_____	_____	_____

Narrative for any items answered yes in column 3:

Developmentally Delayed Form

Obtain or document during the evaluation process:

Face Validity:

1) Test scores that meet the WAC numerical criteria (or your state's criteria) for each area of qualification.
2) The qualification areas must be the noted DD areas: Cognitive Development, Communication Development, Physical Development, Social or Emotional Development, and/or Adaptive Development.
3) General education input that is supportive of qualification (when applicable). Or, for preschool children, in appropriate activities.
4) Explanation and description of adverse impact and need for specially designed instruction (SDI) as related to this specific data.

Language Learning:

5) Documentation of impact of language on all testing (Did the student fully understand the directions? If no, check yes for language impact).
6) For adverse impact, documentation of how language learning and the impacts of the developmental delay are each separately related to the adverse impact.
7) The team has explained (so that a stranger would understand) the impact of exposure, experience, expectations and practice on all areas of noted concern.

<table>
<tr><td>Before the evaluation, ensure that the following were completed:</td></tr>
<tr><td>1) The ELL Critical Data Process was completed by the team and the team agreed that a special education evaluation was needed.
2) School data has been evaluated and processed to show impact (or lack thereof) of school practices on qualification rates of language learners.</td></tr>
</table>

Checklist to Meet the Standard for Developmentally Delayed

	Evidence Documented?		Language Impact?	
	Yes	No	Yes	No
1)	_____	_____	_____	_____
2)	_____	_____	_____	_____
3)	_____	_____	_____	_____
4)	_____	_____	_____	_____
5)	_____	_____	_____	_____
6)	_____	_____	_____	_____
7)	_____	_____	_____	_____

Narrative for any items answered yes in column 3:

Specific Learning Disability Form

Obtain or document during the evaluation process:

<table>
<tr><td>

Face Validity:

1) Academic testing, almost always formal and standardized for discrepancy model. RTI data, if RTI qualification is formally adopted by your district in accordance with state laws, PSW data if using PSW model.
2) Intellectual testing data: either from one recent test, or from two past tests (if using Discrepancy or PSW model), or a solid explanation as to why only one past test (if you are dealing with a re-evaluation), or RTI methodology (if following appropriate legal requirements).

</td>
<td>

Before the evaluation, ensure that the following were completed:

1) The ELL Critical Data Process was completed by the team and the team agreed that a special education evaluation was needed.
2) School data has been evaluated and processed to show impact (or lack thereof) of school practices on qualification rates of language learners.

</td></tr>
</table>

3) Documentation of severe discrepancy if using discrepancy model, or RTI methodology documentation of lack of response to intervention, or documentation of PSW characteristics.
4) Classroom observation in area of concern like reading, math and/or written language (in addition to other observations)
5) General education input that is supportive of qualification.
6) Explanation and description of adverse impact and need for specially designed instruction (SDI) as related to this specific data.

Language Learning:

7) Documentation of impact of language on all testing (Did the student fully understand the directions? If no, check yes for language impact).
8) For adverse impact, documentation of how language learning and the impacts of the specific learning disability are each separately related to the adverse impact.
9) Documentation of learning disability, e.g. information from previous educational setting in student's native language.
10) SLD addendum from the ELL Critical Data Process completed and supportive of qualification.

Checklist to Meet the Standard for Specifically Learning Disability

	Evidence Documented?		Language Impact?	
	Yes	No	Yes	No
1)	_____	_____	_____	_____
2)	_____	_____	_____	_____
3)	_____	_____	_____	_____
4)	_____	_____	_____	_____
5)	_____	_____	_____	_____
6)	_____	_____	_____	_____
7)	_____	_____	_____	_____
8)	_____	_____	_____	_____
9)	_____	_____	_____	_____
10)	_____	_____	_____	_____

Narrative for any items answered yes in column 3:

Appendix B: Sources on Problems in Qualification and Disproportionality

Many of you will be facing a variety of challenges in discussing the appropriate students to evaluate for special education services. You are likely to face a lot of "push back" from your teams. This is due, in part, to people wanting to help children and not seeing other options. Part of convincing people of the necessity of looking for other options involves helping them to understand that the current option is not appropriate for some of our students. That is, if you have disproportionality (and almost everyone does), then some students are not getting the appropriate interventions. The following quotes are meant to help in the creation of new knowledge.

Each of these is directly quoted from the source noted. The source of the information for the following excerpts is listed first. Please refer to the source for further information.

ChildTrends

Child Trends Databank. (2014). Learning disabilities. Available at: http://www.childtrends.org/?indicators=learning-disabilities

> *Differences by Parental Education In 2013, children who had a parent with a Bachelor's degree or higher were less likely to have a learning disability than those with parents who had only a high school diploma or some college...*

> *Children in poverty and in families that receive public assistance are more likely to be identified as having a learning disability.*

Authors' note: What is likely to be the real issue? We suggest the real issue here is that in many cases the students who are overqualified are lacking some of the exposure, experience, expectations and practice, instead of being students with disabilities.

Education Week

Keeping Special Ed in Proportion, by Anthony Rebora, available at: http://www.edweek.org/tsb/articles/2011/10/13/01disproportion.h05.html

> *... African-American students were nearly or greater than twice as likely as white students to be classified with emotional or intellectual disabilities*

> *In other words, there are kids who are placed in these programs because educators either don't want to deal with them, don't know how to deal with them, or don't know how to be responsive to them.*

Scholars generally don't blame racial disproportionality in special education on outright discrimination. Instead, they say it typically derives from systemic flaws within a school or district's instructional culture that allow for some disadvantaged students to fall through the cracks.

Authors' note: What is likely occurring here? The authors suggest that acculturation and a lack of certain knowledge is impacting the decision makers in subtle ways, ways in which they are not aware. They need to see their own data and have some tough conversations to address these problems.

Report to Congress

Information from the *Twenty-fourth Annual Report to Congress on the Implementation of the Individuals with Disabilities Education Act (IDEA)* (U.S. Department of Education, 2002), available at: http://www2.ed.gov/about/reports/annual/osep/2002/index.html

Using data from the U.S. Department of Education, analyses suggest that Black children are 2.88 times more likely than White children to be labeled as having mental retardation and 1.92 times more likely to be labeled as having an emotional/behavioral disorder (Losen & Orfield, 2002). Research suggests that unconscious racial bias, stereotypes, inequitable implementation of discipline policies, and practices that are not culturally responsive may contribute to the observed patterns of identification and placement for many minority students.

Authors' note: What is likely occurring here? Like the authors of this quote said, there is unconscious bias and practices that are not culturally responsible. However, most people will struggle to see this and first need to see their own data to encourage introspection. This can be very hard to hear for the majority group. We need to have the courage for this introspection.

NASP (National Association of School Psychologists)

NASP Communiqué, Vol. 38, #1, September 2009

Multicultural Affairs, Confronting Inequity in Special Education, Part I: Understanding the Problem of Disproportionality, by Amanda L. Sullivan, Elizabeth A'Vant, John Baker, Daphne Chandler, Scott Graves, Edward McKinney, & Tremaine Sayles:

Black students, particularly those identified as mentally retarded or emotionally disabled, have been consistently overrepresented for more than 3 decades. Native American students are also persistently overrepresented in special education nationally, and while the same is not true for Latino students, they are often overrepresented at the state and district levels where their enrollment is highest.

Special education identification patterns vary both between and within states. For instance, risk for Black students identified as mentally retarded is more than 14 times that of their White peers in some states while risk is nearly equivalent in others.

The disproportionality literature tends to focus on the disability categories of mental retardation, learning disabilities, and emotional disabilities, as these are the high-incidence disabilities and constitute over 63% of students eligible for special education (U.S. Department of Education [USDOE], 2009). These are also widely regarded as "judgmental" categories because of relatively vague federal and state disability definitions that necessitate a high degree of professional judgment in making normative comparisons to determine eligibility (Klingner et al., 2005). This has led many to question the validity of these diagnoses as true disabilities and the likelihood of misidentification, particularly in light of the wide variation in identification rates across states and districts. In contrast, diagnoses in the low-incidence categories are rarely challenged because of their physical/medical bases, and because disproportionality is not generally observed in these categories.

Authors' note: What is likely occurring here? The authors want to focus on one portion of this quote that is often forgotten or overlooked. Is it possible to have a disability that appears and disappears depending upon your zip code? No way! Therefore, we need to remember that there are some significant issues regarding how subjective our practices are in these areas. Now, with data, we can work to become more objective. This is not bad people doing bad things, but instead poor practices leading to bad results. We need new practices and new knowledge to get new results. We either created or sustained the bad results, now we can solve the problems and achieve positive results.

Center for Public Education

This examination of special education was prepared for the Center for Public Education by Ulrich Boser, October 15, 2009, available at:

Found at: www.centerforpubliceducatio.org

The complete URL is listed below:

http://www.centerforpubliceducation.org/Main-Menu/Evaluating-performance/Special-education-At-a-glance/Special-education-A-better-perspective-full-report.html

The disparities between whites and some minorities in special education appear mostly in the categories with the most subjective eligibility criteria, such

as "mild mental retardation" or "specific learning disabilities." Many believe the disproportionate representation is due to misconceptions about race and culture, and that Black and Hispanic children are more likely to be misidentified as disabled (Education Week 2004, National Research Council 2002).

For instance, Matthew Ladner and Christopher Hammons argue that race plays an enormously important role in how students are identified as disabled (Ladner and Hammons, 2001). In a study in the book *Rethinking Special Education for a New Century*, they found that in districts with a predominantly Black faculty, there was a reduction in minority student enrollment in special education services by three to four times. "Race," they concluded, "impacts special education rates far more than any other variable.

Authors' note: What is likely occurring here? If the rate in which students are qualified for special education varies in relationship to the race/ethnicity of the teachers, we really need to be willing to look at how our acculturation, knowledge and resulting belief systems are impacting our work. If we are the problem, then we can be the solution. We are loving and good people.

University of Texas at Austin

Education and Transition to Adulthood, Information on Learning Disabilities, available at: http://www.utexas.edu/cola/etag/Related%20Sites/Learning-Disabilities.php

Although the research focus has primarily been on the disproportionate labeling of racial minorities with LD, the research team found that differences in the rates of being labeled are more dramatic by socioeconomic status (SES) than by race. The odds of being labeled with LD are much higher among low SES than high SES high school students, regardless of whether the student is Black or white. In fact, low SES white high school students are as likely as low SES Black or Hispanic high school students to be labeled with LD, but much greater proportions of racial minorities are in that high-risk low SES group.

In contrast to Black and white high school students, high SES Hispanic high school students are as likely as low SES Hispanic high school students to be labeled with LD. The team found that disproportionate labeling of Hispanic students with learning disabilities in high school is attributable to the over-labeling of language minorities.

The team also found that students attending higher poverty schools are actually less likely to be labeled with LD, and that systematic differences in academic achievement by SES, race, and linguistic status are a major factor in disproportionality.

Authors' note: What is likely occurring here? Mathematically there is only a tiny relationship between a student's parents being in poverty (putting the student into poverty) and the possibility that the parent and then the student will have a disability. However, the research is showing poverty as a very high predictor of whether or not a student will be qualified for special education services. Knowing this, each of us needs to understand whether or not this problem is occurring in our school district. Then, if it is occurring, we need to have conversations with everyone involved. Poverty does not create disabilities, but we might be labeling it as such. Use this information to help everyone move to better practices.

Appendix C: Recommended Books

Catherine Collier:

- Separating Difference from Disability

Virginia Collier and Wayne Thomas:

- Dual Language Education for a Transformed World
- Educating English Language Learners for a Transformed World

Carol Dweck

- Mindset: The New Psychology of Success

Steve Gill and Ushani Nanayakkara

- The ELL Critical Data Process – 2nd Edition: Distinguishing Between Disability and Language Acquisition
- Processing Perspective, Examining Beliefs, Biases and Reality Through Stories
- Special Education Referral or Not
- ELL Teachers and Special Education

John Hattie

- Visible Learning: A Synthesis of over 800 Meta-Analyses Related to Achievement

Anthony Muhammed

- Overcoming the Achievement Gap Trap

Robert Rhodes, Salvador Hector Ochoa, and Samuel Ortiz

- Assessing Culturally and Linguistically Diverse Students

Appendix D: Steve Gill Biography and Training

Steve Gill Biography

Steve's first job in education, before he became a school psychologist, was as a driver's education teacher. Then Steve had a wonderful opportunity to study school psychology and work at the university, so he followed that path.

Steve started his career as a school psychologist in a district with a large ELL population. There he realized how little he had learned about language learners prior to this experience. Over the years, he completed graduate work in ELL studies, eventually creating the ELL Critical Data Process. As of writing this, Steve has trained over 9,000 educators on the process across more than 200 school districts in multiple states.

Steve and Ushani (Steve's wife and co-author) have five books for sale on Amazon.com. The first book, *The ELL Critical Data Process - Second Edition,* is a resource for learning professionals for determining whether more interventions are needed or if a special education referral is a reasonable option. Their second book, *Evaluating ELL Students for the Possibility of Special Education Qualification – Second Edition* focuses on the special education evaluation process for language learners and how to potentially achieve appropriate identification rates. The third book, *Special Education Referral or Not*, is about using a matrix based approach with non-language learners. *ELL Teachers and Special Education*, the fourth book, is a self-study or group study for ELL teachers to learn more about special education. Their fifth book, *Processing Perspective, Examining Beliefs, Biases and Reality Through Stories*, uses educator stories to help people see different perspectives and analyze the lens we each look through to view the world.

Steve is currently the President of the Washington State Association of School Psychologists.

Training

Steve Gill is available to provide 1 to 4-day training sessions on ELL and special education issues. For more information, please go to www.stevegillell.com.

Feedback on Trainings, Process, and Books

Diversity and Social Justice Training Feedback

"I'd like to take this opportunity to thank you again for sharing your expertise with our members on March 21st at the Diversity and Social Justice Conference. As you can see from the feedback below, the participants were filled with insights and inspiration that will affect their practice. We appreciate your consideration to return as a speaker as we plan future offerings. Thank you!!   C."

District Training Feedback:

"When you sit through one of Steve's Data Matrix trainings, it becomes extremely clear how much school districts have lacked the expertise and methods for carrying out referrals and evaluations on students who are English Language Learners. I personally learned more in the 2-hour session about English Language Learners than I ever did in graduate school or my own practice. His work is thorough, eye-opening, and most importantly, practical." AG, School Psychologist

"Steve uses research based content and district data in his presentation with both care and humor. He is conscientious to both recognize the passion of educators, while working to move them forward in their practice of evaluating students from second language backgrounds. This is such an important topic for staff and Steve's work is critical in helping to move our district forward in this area. The protocol that Steve has developed should be required of any team evaluating an ELL student for possible special education eligibility." KH, Asst. Director of Special Education

"Steve's presentation was clear, concise and built on foundational principles of Special Education, Civil Rights, and the science of language learning and was immediately relevant to the real work that we do every day as school practitioners facing complicated questions. His training and material was the catalyst that launched our district on a path toward more informed interventions for culturally and linguistically diverse students." BC, Special Services Coordinator

"Your book is wonderful--a very much needed resource in an area of great need. Thanks for sending us a copy! Although we are not specialists in special education, we have done enough work with doctoral graduates who are bilingual special ed. experts to know that your book has a system for appropriate assessment that is very much more comprehensive than anything else we have seen to date. Wow, you have reached many educators in the state of Washington through this training and providing this book to them! And you can indeed be proud of your work, reducing the number of English learners assessed as needing special education services, across the state of Washington." VC, Professor, Researcher, Author

"Dear …,

I wanted to write to you to tell you how invaluable Steve Gill's training was for our District yesterday. He presented to 63 staff members who sit on our building Guidance Teams: Principals, Deans of Students, School Counselors, School Psychologists, and Speech/Language Pathologists. He presented for a full day on ELL and Special Education and then remained for extra time to offer examples and specific guidance for the process he has developed to our school psychologists. He was a compelling speaker, he easily engaged and held the attention of all of the participants. He cited research and used data throughout. He used our own District data to inform us about how we are addressing dually identified students (ELL/IDEA) in our District providing us a road map for improvement. I want to thank you for allowing Steve to bring this important knowledge and practice to other Districts.

Thanks so much, on behalf of our staff, and especially, our students."

SW, Special Education Director

Made in the USA
San Bernardino, CA
15 May 2020